Skira Rizzoli

BALENCIAGA AND SPAIN

HAMISH BOWLES

Fine Arts Museums of San Francisco

Skira Rizzoli
NEW YORK

Published by the Fine Arts Museums of San Francisco and
Skira Rizzoli Publications, Inc., on the occasion of the exhibition
Balenciaga and Spain, on view at the de Young Museum from
March 26 through July 4, 2011.

Balenciaga and Spain was organized by the Fine Arts Museums
of San Francisco.

PLATINUM SPONSORS
San Francisco Auxiliary of the Fine Arts Museums
Christine Suppes

GOLD SPONSOR

Neiman Marcus

The catalogue is published with the assistance of the Andrew W. Mellon
Foundation Endowment for Publications.

Text by Baroness Philippe de Rothschild reproduced by kind
permission of The Metropolitan Museum of Art, The Irene Lewisohn
Costume Reference Library, Designer Files. Images copyright
© The Metropolitan Museum of Art, New York.

Additional photography and copyright credits appear on page 256.

First published in the United States in 2011 by

Skira Rizzoli Publications, Inc.
300 Park Avenue South
New York, NY 10010
www.rizzoliusa.com

Fine Arts Museums of San Francisco
Golden Gate Park
50 Hagiwara Tea Garden Drive
San Francisco, CA 94118-4502
www.famsf.org

2011 2012 2013 2014 / 10 9 8 7 6 5 4 3 2 1

Distributed in the U.S. trade by Random House, New York

Cataloging-in-Publication Data is available from the Library of Congress
Library of Congress Control Number: 2010047715

ISBN 978-0-8478-3646-8 (hardcover)
ISBN 978-0-88401-132-3 (paperback)

DESIGNED BY
AR New York

Printed in China

COVER
Evening bolero jacket of blood-red silk velvet with jet and
passementerie embroidery by Bataille, winter 1946
Collection of Hamish Bowles
Photo by Kenny Komer

CONTENTS

DIRECTOR'S FOREWORD

John E. Buchanan, Jr.

It is with great pride and excitement that the Fine Arts Museums of San Francisco present *Balenciaga and Spain*, a captivating look at the influence of Cristóbal Balenciaga's native land—from its rich artistic tradition to its distinctive regional cultures—on his extraordinary designs.

It is a project that is several years in the making. The seed of its idea was planted in the fall of 2008, when *Vogue's* European editor at large, Hamish Bowles, participated in a symposium hosted by the de Young in conjunction with *Yves Saint Laurent*. Hamish captivated us with his deep and passionate knowledge of couture, and we began to imagine collaborating together on the next big costume exhibition for Bay Area audiences.

We were enormously pleased when Hamish suggested that the de Young become a venue for *Balenciaga: Spanish Master*, an exhibition that the renowned designer Oscar de la Renta had invited him to organize for the Queen Sofia Spanish Institute in New York. Although the San Francisco exhibition has ultimately grown into a much larger presentation with an expanded focus, we are grateful to Mr. de la Renta, Inmaculada de Habsburgo, and their colleagues at the Queen Sofia for stimulating this important project.

Every great master deserves major museum exhibitions to achieve a full assessment of his or her oeuvre, and Balenciaga is no exception. It has often been noted that his designs bear the indelible impression of Spanish culture, but never before have his Iberian influences been traced in such a thorough and compelling way. Hamish Bowles is surely one of the brightest minds working in fashion today, and I can imagine no better guide to lead us through the story of Balenciaga's inspirations: the paintings by Velázquez, Goya, and Picasso; the elaborately worked gowns and armor of the royal court; the garb of cardinals, monks, and Madonnas; the flourish and ruffles of flamenco dance; the ritual theatricality of the bullring; and the colorful costumes found in villages throughout Spain's many regions. Hamish has done an astounding job in sourcing the looks for the exhibition, and his contacts in the fashion world are certainly unmatched. With unflagging energy and enthusiasm, he has identified the finest Balenciaga examples the world over. On behalf of everyone at the Fine Arts Museums, I thank him for his partnership on this exhibition and congratulate him on his achievement.

All of our most successful special exhibitions have roots in the Museums' permanent collections. This one naturally draws on the strengths of the Fine Arts Museums' costume holdings, containing several exquisite Balenciaga designs once worn by San Francisco's most well-heeled women, including Mrs. C. H. Russell, Eleanor Christensen de Guigne, and Elise S. Haas. But the exhibition would have been unthinkable without the cooperation and generosity of the house of Balenciaga, most notably François Pinault, founder of PPR; François-Henri Pinault, CEO of PPR; and Nicolas Ghesquière, creative director of Balenciaga Paris. Balenciaga's Lionel Vermeil and Gaël Mamine facilitated unprecedented access to the archives, the loan of a tremendous number of landmark designs, and many of the fascinating documentary images that grace the pages of this volume. Thomas Campbell, Harold Koda, and Andrew Bolton at the Metropolitan Museum of Art, New York, are also deserving of special thanks. The exhibition includes remarkable ensembles on loan from museum and private collections throughout the United States and Europe, and we are grateful to all of our lenders for their assistance and participation.

A project of this scope and complexity can only be possible with the generous support of the Museums' patrons. We are enormously grateful to those who have made early leadership gifts to underwrite this exhibition: Christine Suppes, the San Francisco Auxiliary of the Fine Arts Museums, and Neiman Marcus.

I know Hamish joins me in thanking the hard-working and capable staff of the Fine Arts Museums for their many contributions to the project. Jill D'Alessandro, curator of costume and textiles, was essential to the exhibition from its inception, serving as Hamish's crucial liaison to San Francisco, facilitating access to the Museums' collections and resources, and lending her expertise in mounting exhibitions. Karen Levine, director of publications, has overseen the catalogue with flexibility and aplomb. Krista Brugnara, director of exhibitions, handled logistics with an array of international lenders, adeptly aided by Therese Chen, Leni Velasquez, and Suzy Peterson. The project has also been shaped by the vital input of textile conservators Sarah Gates and Beth Szuhay, who cared for and participated in the dressing of these delicate costumes; Susan Grinols and Joseph McDonald, whose work resulted in stunning new photography of the Museums' Balenciaga pieces; and Sheila Pressley and Renée Baldocchi, who spearheaded the symposium and other educational offerings. Warmest gratitude is owed to Bill White, Steve Brindmore, and the technical production staff as well as the marketing and design team. Recognition is also due to Hamish's research assistants, Jennifer Park and Molly Sorkin, for their tireless efforts on behalf of the project.

Acknowledgments concluded, we turn to a poignant appreciation of Balenciaga written the year after his death by one of his greatest patrons, Baroness Philippe de Rothschild. And, thus our journey begins in Guetaria, the maestro's birthplace on the Basque coast.

1
Richard Avedon
Dorian Leigh wearing evening ensemble of black silk organza
and white cotton piqué, summer 1951
Variant originally published in *Harper's Bazaar*, April 1951

2
Horst P. Horst
Pauline de Rothschild wearing coat of black lace and brown organza, winter 1953
Originally published in *Vogue*, July 1, 1963

BALENCIAGA, appreciation by Baroness Philippe de Rothschild

In the center of a street, made dark by the shadows of it's thick stone houses, a woman was walking, her back turned to the light from the sea. She wore a pale, ankle-length, silk shantung suit. The severe houses enclosed her, shuttered.

A boy was watching her.

She would come almost abreast of him, and he would run up a side-street of the fishing village, so closely carved into the mountain that it's streets are as steep and narrow as Genoa's, some entirely made of steps. Down another he would run and be ahead of her again.

Then he would stare.

One day he stopped her, and asked her if he could make a suit for her. The boy was about thirteen, with dark hair and darker eyes and the smile he would keep all his life.

- Why do you want to do this? she asked.

- Because I think I can, he answered.

The boy was Cristobal Balenciaga.

The woman was the Marquesa de Casa Torres. We know nothing of the outcome of the first attempt. The Marquesa had him begin the long years of apprenticeship to his trade. In Spain, then, some say, in Bordeaux. When he was eighteen she took him to Paris to see Mr. Doucet. Mr. Doucet was a great collector, and a very grand dressmaker. The boy saw how Caroline ReGoux's hats were brought over for each fitting, how one fussed about proportions. Years later the Marquesa, still infinitely fashionable, insisted that the young man open his own house in Madrid. The Spanish civil war (the siege of Madrid lasted eighteen months), brought him to Paris. The rest is not only the history of his clothes, but that of mysteries particularly his own.

I had the privilege of dressing at Balenciaga's for twenty-three years. I knew and loved other dressmakers, and understood them. But the mysteries were Balenciaga's.

He exerted a close to total dominance over his field. He did his own thing, as the saying goes, and where sayings cannot go, he went. His own way. Intransigeant in his creativeness, in his dealings with people, with a sway over the very bones and minds of those who wore his clothes. Perhaps even over their flesh. The women wearing a dress of his, or a coat, or a raincoat, seemed to have acquired a birth-certificate to some commitment of their own secret choosing. And of his. One night, he never went to galas or to a party, was never seen in restaurants or the theatre, he refused to let a dress be delivered to one of his most beautiful and favorite clients, a dress ordered to be worn that very evening at one of three receptions in Paris for the Queen of England. The dress had been changed, he said. He did not like what had been done to it. It would be put in the sales, but not until it had been brought back to it's original conception. (The crime consisted of sewing the seams of a dress down to the floor, instead of letting it be two panels opening over a tunic). The saleswoman responsible would pay for the alteraions out of her own money. "I didn't mind the money", later moaned the saleswoman, "but imagine not being able to deliver the dress'. "

Where had he developed this sureness?

His name became synonymous with perfection and elegance. Why these two words, in themselves unexplainable? How does the Oxford dictionary explain perfection? It gives, as an illustration,: "The hawk that is most suited for the flight." Perhaps. And elegance? "Neatness, grace, raffinement." No. There must be some cuckoo's eggs in the nest.

Where did he train his eyes to choose and limit his colors so that each became a rarity? As subtle and firm as that of the most sparing of Chinese painters. This man who only travelled between France ans Spain.

And the ever-renewed sciende of cutting? The superb cut that engendered a serentiy in movement, a look of ceremonial. Where did he learn this? Not in any appreaticeship.

There was the magnificence too, the adventures dirtthe evening, for the night.

From Goya, of course, came the prettimiess of black lace and satin ribbbns, but what of the spumes of frosted embroiderjes, the showers of mother-of-pearl, the pale slightly-stiffened silks layered in silver and gold so that you did not know which moved first, the dress or the light? There was onee a bolero emrbtoidered in natural straw the color of Inca gold.

So, one day in February, we waht on a pilgrimage of affection and admiration to Guetaria, on the Northern coast of Spain, where Balenciaga was born and where he asked to have his body buried. It was an atlantic winter day, suöden bursts of sun, then rapid clouds. The houses on the mainsstreet, their heavy stone still wet from the rain, glistened as if covered with a gold metallic armor. The proprietors of these seuenteenth century houses are well-tê-do. Their boats sail out in the spring to the Arctic seas, to Iceland, for dod-fishing. A map in a recent edition of Moby Dick shows that whales had a visiting place very near and directly facing Guetaria. In the church, we were to see two pews, to be iddatified by the carvings of two very small whales, harpooned, each surmounted by a cross. Whalers and believers. Visibly, a people of pride and nimbleness.

The cemetary lies on the side of a hill like a sheet spread out to dry. Vineyards run down to it. Balenciaga's tomb is the highest of two Balenciaga family plots, looking out toward the vineyards and the sea and one lone beautiful pine tree. Balenciaga's tomb is particularly ugly. Slab upon slab of grey granit, and a standing head-board of granit topped by ill-shaped cross. It promises total blindness and deafness. Solid, expensive, it needs no upkeep, no gestures of fondness, it doesn't allow for weeds. What is he doing there, the austere voluptuary who so often gave us Cinderella's three dresses, one the color of the weather, the other the color of the moon, the third the color of the morning sun? He would be happier with the poor, further down, lucky to lie under the green grass and who only require black cast-iron crosses of delicate patterns with the green of the grass showing through.

But look carefully at the vineyards which he must have seen so often. The tutors of the vines show that they have a difficult time of it as they are so heavily sprayed with copper sulfate. And as you look you see the swatches of a Balenciaga collection: rain washed blues, greys with a greenish tinge, the weather has in places washed the dark brown wood to pale coffee, to white, and sometimes left a harsh metallic blue. No Mediterranean colors these, no red earth, no sapphire sea. The eye that chooses so much for us knew the beauty of black hulls in Atlantic mists, black against egg-shell, against brown. The boats and their sails.

A sail is hung from a very precise point so that it will resist or give to the pressure of the wind. The shape of the sail determines the amount of yielding. It is mathematically constructed to respond ;to respond to certain conditions. I had had in my hands a few days ago a magazine on sailing and had marvelled at photographs of sail-boats almost becalmed with sails of all shapes and colors, rounding out, fitted to hold the slightest breeze.in a seemingless windless hour, the sails were kept shaped and alive.

A woman walking would displace the air so that her skirt would billow out just so much, front and back and sides would round out each in turn, imperceptably, like a sea-swell.

That was the answer to these miracles of cut, the black tulips he would send out across the floor. Nothing held them out, neither whalebone cages or petticoats gave them any support. Legs moved easily, the front of the long skirt running a little faster ahead than one's walk, like the tides, you were given the elements, you could use them at will. This created never cared much where the breasts were placed. "Monsieur Balenciaga likes a little stomach" the fitter would say. One afternoon, the waist disappeared altogether.

As for the general look achieved (for a long time, before the sack and the tunic) he preferred, as does Japanese art, the horizontal to the vertical. His clothes took on great width. They sometimes looked to me like a group of great insects with outspread wings when in reality they were closer to Japanese stage clothes.

Wit was on the head, where it should be, and several seasons saw small impertinent black velvet hats with a straight tab up their back, such as those of long gone Japanese gentlemen, shōguns impertubable under their highly lacquered head gear. On August sixth in Guetaria they hold the feast of Juan Sebastian Elcano, "the first navigator to circle around the world", in five years 1519 to 1523. There in his birthplace, they play out his trip and his return. Which brings us back to procession and Balenciaga's four and six sided dresses like Spanish madonnas'. This brings back splendor. Perhaps the church would bring an answer.

Too big for the town, it stands across the end of the main street, a tawny animal high on it's legs, arching it's back and stomach over a paved road where eight horses could have stood abreast. The road runs down to the warfs below, straight through the walled-up crypt. In summer all manner of craft sail into the triangular port, and people walk up through the cool arch into the shadows of the street. They eat sardines grilled on iron grills the size of ship births. Inside the church, the madonna in a long hooded black cloak was there, the silver handles of the seren swords of our deadly sins stuck through her heart.

A smaller madonna is carried in processions. The vehemence of her usual ornamentation had disappeared, perhaps with the civil war, and she was soberly clad, just a few sequins on a discolored dress, but the shape was there. Not much splendor. Other cathedrals not too far away must have furnished this, Burgos for instance or the exquisite Miraflores with it's double octagon that encloses king and queen, as the poet tells us. Because Balenciaga used splendor as if he could make it materialize our the shining things that man has invented to distract and possess, gold, diamonds, mirrors and their like. He, Balenciaga, worked as if he wished to annul the dark, the perishable, the disillysion-ment. It was uhintellectual, and very straightforward, made to last forever. There was voluptuousness, and wit, and severity.

We are in front of a monumental work, in itself a pilgrimage. Pilgrimages give unexpected rewards. Geetaria holds many of Cristobal Balenciaga's reasons. Though it is dangerous to try, if notimpossible to invade the privacy of a man's genius. Errors set in. Yet one knows that imprints in the eye come up to it's surface. At the end, some said the collections were not as bold, no longer prophetic. Then he made one, the one before-last. It was the collection of a very young man together with all the knowledge.

In Spanish, the verb to wish, to want, to love is one and the same. Tu quières ? Perhaps at the beginning of life, at thirteen, one should ask only that question of others and of oneself.

Pauline de Rothschild
February 1973

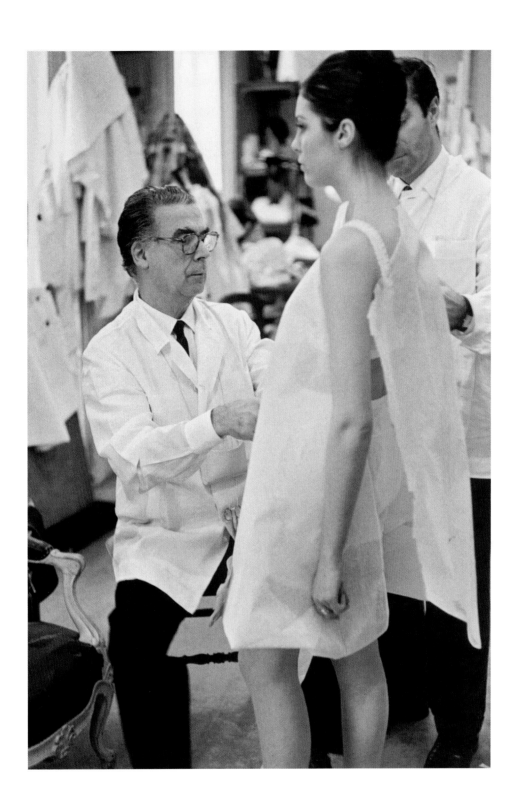

3

Henri Cartier-Bresson
Cristóbal Balenciaga fitting the mannequin Nina, Paris, 1968

INTRODUCTION

Hamish Bowles

For three fecund decades, from 1937 until 1968, Cristóbal Balenciaga honed and perfected the art and craft of the haute couture from his monastic ateliers on the avenue George V in the heart of fashionable Paris. His fascination with the properties of cloth—its cut, construction, and embellishment—and his inventive responses to its possibilities established him from the beginning as a master of his métier (to use his preferred term).[1]

Balenciaga's ceaseless explorations and innovations ensured that his work was as intriguing and influential in his final collections as it had been in his first. Indeed, in many ways he reversed the designer's traditional career trajectory, producing some of his most thoughtful and even provocative designs in the twilight of his career.

His talent led him to create a body of work that garnered the approbation of his peers, the plaudits of the press, and considerable financial rewards. Christian Dior applauded his "creative genius"[2] and crowned him "the master of us all."[3] *Harper's Bazaar*'s influential editor Carmel Snow called him "the greatest name in fashion." His buyers and clients ranked among the preeminent tastemakers of the day. In 1959, his fashion house had the highest profit margin in the couture, although Dior had six times as many employees.[4]

Although Paris, with its craftspeople and *fournisseurs* of brilliance, provided the ideal setting for Balenciaga to perfect his craft, it was his native Spain that cast the longest shadow. As the legendary fashion editor Diana Vreeland noted, Balenciaga "brought the style of Spain into the lives of everyone who wore his designs." For Vreeland, "Balenciaga was the true son of a strong country filled with style, vibrant color, and a fine history," who "remained forever a Spaniard. . . . His inspiration came from the bullrings, the flamenco dancers, the fishermen in their boots and loose blouses, the glories of the church and the cool of the cloisters and monasteries. He took their colors, their cuts, then festooned them to his own taste."[5]

Balenciaga spent two decades in his native Spain, establishing his name and reputation as a tailor, dressmaker, and designer of distinction and creating a fashion empire with couture salons in Madrid, Barcelona, and San Sebastián. However, the traumatic upheavals of the Spanish Civil War forced him to flee, and he eventually reestablished himself in Paris, where he opened his eponymous couture house in 1937.[6] In France the potent influences of Spanish art, culture, religion, and history continued to inform his work for the next thirty years, building up "a picture of a man homesick for his own land to whom visual memories keep returning," as fashion historian Colin McDowell has observed.[7] This Spanish influence characterized Balenciaga's work—and the way it was perceived and documented by the press—for the rest of his career. In 1938 *Harper's Bazaar* commented, "Balenciaga projects a new quality into the couture, a definite personality into the fray. There's a flavor of Spain about his whole collection."[8]

As evidenced by his color palette, Balenciaga believed "in the unquestionable elegance of black and white, in the color of the Spanish earth and rocks and olive trees, in the red of the bull ring, in the effective accent of turquoise, in the Goya combination of black with beige, gray with black, and in yellow."[9] A particular shade of cinnamon was known as "Balenciaga brown." As noted by José María de Areilza, the Spanish ambassador to the United States from 1954 to 1960, "the dark browns and blacks that we see in Antoni Tàpies's paintings were often used and combined" in Balenciaga's work.[10] But these are also the background colors in Francisco de Zurbarán's haunting seventeenth-century images of saints, Diego Velázquez's portraits of courtiers and royalty, and Juan Sánchez Cotán's still-life studies of humble vegetables—God's creations all, celebrated and ennobled in their unworldly isolation.

During the first half of Balenciaga's Paris career, the Spanish influence on his work was overt; his designs referenced widely recognizable tropes such as the *bata de cola* (dress with a ruffled train) of the flamenco dancer and, although he disliked bullfights, the nineteenth-century matador's *traje de luces* (suit of

Boris Lipnitzki
Cristóbal Balenciaga, France, 1927

lights).[11] "In his collection there is always an echo of his native land," wrote *Harper's Bazaar* in 1948, "an evocation of the Spain of brilliant colors, beads, paillettes, pompoms, and the little jacket of the matador." Balenciaga's evening clothes from this period often suggest the hieratic costume and even the headdresses of Velázquez's infantas as well as the coquettish dress and accoutrements of Francisco de Goya's *majas*. In Balenciaga's youth, the black lace mantilla worn by Goya's aristocratic sitters in the late eighteenth century was still de rigueur for Catholic mass and for religious festivals and processions throughout the year.[12]

For his winter 1939 collection Balenciaga created a series of evening gowns (pls. 5, 30) directly inspired by Velázquez's portraits of the Infanta Margarita and her ladies-in-waiting (see pl. 29). For *Harper's Bazaar*, George Hoyningen-Huene photographed two of these gowns against canvases by Pablo Picasso and sculptures by Constantin Brancusi in the Île Saint-Louis apartment of the beauty industry entrepreneur Helena Rubinstein, who became an important Balenciaga client.[13]

In 1939 the International Committee for the Safeguarding of Spanish Art, composed of directors from some of the world's most prestigious art institutions, organized the rescue of masterworks from the Museo Nacional del Prado and other notable collections.[14] The resulting exhibition opened at the Musée d'Art et d'Histoire in Geneva on June 4, 1939, after receiving consent from the Nationalist government.[15] The display captured the imagination of the public and of many of Balenciaga's fellow couturiers.[16] "Through room after room of Geneva's largest galleries they sweep through the richly hued panorama of … Spanish earth and Spanish heaven," wrote the *New York Times* of the visitors who thronged to the exhibition. "The white walls glow with a splendor of kings and infantas, beggars and dwarfs, monks and madonnas, saints, angels and holy families."[17] Hearing of the Geneva exhibition while en route to the Paris collections, Snow changed her travel plans to accommodate a trip there, where she realized that she was seeing Balenciaga's inspirations before her.[18]

For Cecil Beaton, "Balenciaga was fashion's Picasso."[19] The designer may not have coveted Picasso's work, but it was seared onto the Spanish consciousness. The centerpiece of the Spanish Pavilion of the 1937 World's Fair in Paris, Picasso's *Guernica*, presented by the Republican government—by then ranged against the forces of Germany and Italy as well as the Nationalist forces of General Francisco Franco—drew international attention to the civil war.[20] Like Picasso, Balenciaga, as Richard Martin has noted, "began his art in Spain but practiced it to perfection in France."[21] "Spain is stamped indelibly on the souls of its children," wrote *Life* in a 1968 issue dedicated to Picasso. "A hard and bony landscape, a people dirt-poor and aristocratic, mystical and earthy, generous and intolerant, cruel and compassionate, loving laughter and wild music and so obsessed with mortality that they cloak their lives in mourning and rehearse their deaths on holidays by the ritual slaughter of bulls—this is the nation whose complex nature has given its artists an endless theme."[22]

Dance was also very much a part of the Spanish identity. In the 1920s a movement of Spanish cultural figures and intellectuals had embraced the inherent poignancy of flamenco dance, which, with its plaintive musical accompaniment and songs, was a symbol of the enduring persecution of, and discrimination against, the Gypsies. At the vanguard of the movement, the poet Federico García Lorca had helped to promote the dance's revival.[23] Earlier, Sergey Diaghilev, delighted by the enthusiastic reception accorded his Ballets Russes during a Spanish tour in 1916 and by the subsequent patronage of King Alfonso XIII, had worked with the choreographer Léonide Massine to develop the Spanish-themed ballet *Las meninas*, taking its title from that of Velázquez's famous painting. He also collaborated with the composer Manuel de Falla (whom he had met in Madrid) on the Picasso-designed ballet *Le tricorne*, its music inspired by Spanish folk-dance motifs.[24] Balenciaga also captured this zeitgeist and the ensuing cultural engagement with the visual aspects of flamenco dance. Throughout his career he would continue to abstract the form of the *bata de cola*, with its characteristic ruffles and tiers of fabric, and even that of the male flamenco dancer's costume, with its abbreviated tailored jacket and cummerbund.

Spain's dictator Franco later seized on flamenco dance—detached from its visceral origins—as a tourist attraction. He also saw the drama of the bullfight and the quaint variants of his country's regional dress as seductive and apolitical imagery he could exploit to promote his country's identity on the world stage.[25] Images of flamenco costumes had been disseminated since the eighteenth century (in publications such as *Colección de trajes de España de 1777* and *Colección general de los trajes que en la actualidad se usan en España, principiada en el año 1801 en Madrid*), and they continued to pique international interest into the mid-twentieth century through a variety of media, including potent photographs by José Ortiz-Echagüe, posters, postcards, and even examples of the costumes themselves.[26]

Elements of regional dress such as the sweeping capes of the elders of Ávila; the fichus and scarves of Alicante, Murcia, and La Coruña (among others); the pleated skirts of Cáceres and Toledo; and the rich appliqués of Zamora and Salamanca were still widely prevalent in the years before 1937 when Balenciaga was traveling around Spain, and all find echoes in the designer's work.[27] By turns these garments recall costume traditions from the eighteenth and early nineteenth centuries. From the eighteenth century onward, aristocratic Spanish women had adopted elements of working-class *maja* costume.[28] Anton Raphael Mengs's portrait of the Marquesa de Llano (ca. 1773; pl. 6), for instance, depicts a fashionable woman in a striking black-and-white costume that is interpretative of the dress of a contemporary *maja*, which, in turn, is reflected in Balenciaga's summer 1951 ensemble of a white piqué overdress with an underdress of black organza, its skirts decorated with feathery petals (pls. 1, 7). Balenciaga also used elements of regional dress as a surprising foil for conventional garments, as in the face-encircling bonnet, apparently derived from those worn in festivals in Salamanca, that accessorizes a severely tailored black day suit from the winter 1951 collection (see pls. 8–9). The carnation, the national

5
Eric (Carl Erickson)
"Infanta" evening dress of pink silk satin and black silk velvet
Originally published in *Vogue*, September 15, 1939

16

flower of Spain–thrown in tribute at the feet of the victorious matador and embroidered on religious vestments and altar cloths–is a constantly recurring motif in Balenciaga's fabric and embroidery choices.

In the second half of his Paris career, Balenciaga's experiments with structure and form became ever more audacious, innovative, and abstract. In his winter 1951 collection, for instance, he introduced the unfitted middy blouse, followed by the semifitted suit (summer 1952), the tunic dress (summer 1955), and the A-line baby-doll dress (summer 1958). From this period until his retirement in 1968, the Spanish references, still fundamental to his work, became increasingly oblique. In 1962, for instance, the "national strain" originally cited by *Harper's Bazaar* in 1938 was revealed "in evening gowns with stiffened, shaped ruffles of intense, unfluttery poise."[29] In Balenciaga's hands, these ruffles were more than decorative flourishes; they were integral to the silhouette of the garment. "A ruffle must be intelligent," as the designer told his friend and protégé Hubert de Givenchy.[30]

The coruscations of the *traje de luces* are suggested in beaded embroideries of plastic and Rhodoïd (the brand name for a material similar to celluloid), and their *machos* (tassels) are isolated from their original purpose and used instead as decorative elements on a cape or a playful hat (see pls. 146, 150).[31] The stiff silver galloon bows of a seventeenth-century infanta's headdress are scattered over a columnar evening gown (pl. 73). And the airy volumes of a *robe à la polonaise* punctuated with bows, like that worn by the sitter in Goya's *Marquesa de Pontejos* (ca. 1786; pl. 41), are suggested in the puffball silhouette of a ball gown (pl. 40) made from Lamarre's aléoutienne, a textured silk gauze that was one of the many innovative fabrics whose properties and possibilities Balenciaga relished exploring.

In Balenciaga's work from this period we see the wind-furled sails of the boats departing from the harbor of Guetaria, the all-enveloping costumes of the *cobijadas* of Vejer de la Frontera–so suggestive of the era of Moorish rule of Al-Andalus (711–1492)– and the extraordinary draperies in the statues of the saints and the Holy Family that surrounded the altar of Guetaria's San Salvador, Balenciaga's childhood church, or that billow around those same figures depicted in the paintings of El Greco, Zurbarán, and Bartolomé Esteban Murillo. The vestments of Spain's Catholic Church hierarchy also inform the work of a man who once contemplated following his uncle Julian Balenciaga into the priesthood and who remained profoundly religious throughout his life.[32] The copes, albs, and chasubles of his country's cardinals, bishops, monks, and village priests; the wimples and habits of its nuns; and even the magnificent robes that garb the statues of the Madonna carried through the streets during Holy Week: all achieve sculptural magnificence and authoritative presence through uncomplicated form and minimal seaming that betray their medieval origins. These effects characterize Balenciaga's experiments in the 1960s, when his pursuit of ever more reductive treatments rendered in innovative fabrics (many of which were developed especially for him) resulted in sophisticated and dramatic garments that are constructed with a minimum of seams–or, on occasion, a single seam.

In 1968, the year that Balenciaga closed his house, his friend Gustave Zumsteg (of the Swiss fabric house Abraham) noted that the designer was "as interested in what modern life has to offer us as in the cultural riches of the past, and it is this openness that gives him his strength on the professional and artistic level."[33] In Balenciaga's work from the last decade of his career, one is increasingly aware of his interest in exploring the sculptural potential of clothing. One sees the abstractions of Joan Miró's automatist paintings of the 1920s and even the sturdy volutes of his friend Eduardo Chillida's sculptures in his modernist silhouettes. Balenciaga's friendship with the distinguished collectors Aimé and Marguerite Maeght brought him into close contact with a circle of contemporary artists that included Alberto Giacometti, Miró, Georges Braque, and Marc Chagall.[34]

Balenciaga's experiments in abstraction were counterpointed by his pragmatic ability to provide his clients–and the store buyers and manufacturers who paid hefty premiums for the right to copy or interpret his designs–with the kind of clothes whose quiet evolution of line ensured that they could be worn for years. "Leading U.S.A. buyers will say a Balenciaga suit copy can be sold season after season without changes," commented *Women's Wear Daily (WWD)* on July 9, 1958. "Few other couturiers offer such permanence in fashion."[35] "He has destroyed the time element in fashion," wrote British *Vogue* in 1962. "What Balenciaga designed in 1938 looks uncannily right today."[36] In 1959 *WWD* stated, "Balenciaga believes that an elegant woman does not necessarily wear the latest style, but dresses in a manner becoming to herself, choosing clothes of good material and cut which she wears for several years, changing accessories to make them up-to-date. She never wears clothes that are conspicuous or uncomfortable, is never dominated by fashion, but uses it to express her own personality."[37] For a ball in 1964, Claudia Heard de Osborne, who was relatively fearless in her choice of Balenciaga's more advanced models (that is, the prototype runway designs), nevertheless ordered a gown of black velvet that was based on a silhouette he had shown a decade earlier.[38]

Gabrielle "Coco" Chanel described her friend Balenciaga as "the only couturier. He is the only one who knows how to cut a fabric, and mount it and sew it with his own hands. The others are just draughtsmen."[39] Bettina Ballard, who would become a great friend of Balenciaga's, left us a revealing portrait of the designer in her 1960 autobiography *In My Fashion*. Then a Paris-based fashion editor for American *Vogue*, Ballard ordered a little black dress from the designer's first Paris collection in 1937 and was astonished to discover that he "fitted it himself, impatiently taking the scissors from the fitter and slashing the dress up the front in the most terrifying manner, then pinning it so perfectly that I never had to have it fitted again."[40] In the unfinished 1939 "Infanta" dress in the collection of the Archives Balenciaga, Paris, the bodice has been mounted on its original toile, its penciled inscriptions revealing it to be the handiwork of the designer himself. When he retired, as Givenchy recalls, his doctor encouraged him to knead a piece of putty in his hands to assuage the rheumatism that had developed from decades spent manually shaping cloth to a body. And his perfectionism was legendary. "He has been known to send back most of the collection because it doesn't satisfy him, a few days before the showing date," reported *WWD*. "It doesn't matter if the showing is postponed. Balenciaga wants his models perfect or nothing at all."[41]

Balenciaga's technical skill was honed during the twenty years he spent establishing and developing his three fashion houses in Spain. Much of his work was shaped by personal contact with his patrician and bourgeois clientele and by his responses to their exigent demands. As a result, no less an authority than Vreeland could declare, "He was the master tailor, the master dressmaker."[42] Balenciaga also developed a keen sense of his clients' lifestyles and of the situations for which their clothes were intended, which in Spain at that time revolved around a highly formalized calendar of religious festivals and gala events. As *Harper's Bazaar* observed in 1948, Spain's elite "enjoy tremendous wealth and privilege. Their society, one of the most glittering in Europe, is also a last outpost of the feudal tradition."[43] This direct contact with clients also provided Balenciaga with an innate understanding of what would flatter their bodies. His instinctive command of proportion meant that his clothes looked effective on women of all shapes and sizes. Clients whose figures suggested the contemporary ideal—such as the chic Marquesa de Llanzol, the slim and elegant Gloria Guinness, and the athletic Doris Duke (whose broad shoulders Balenciaga admired)—might order the same ensembles as the diminutive Elizabeth Parke Firestone and screenwriter Anita Loos or the Junoesque Princess Nina Mdivani and Fern Bedaux. Regardless, their Balenciaga clothing would lend each of these women an air of natural distinction. Balenciaga's tricks of proportion meant, for instance, that the clothes made on Taiga, Balenciaga's star mannequin of the late 1950s and 1960s, fit Loos (at four feet eleven inches).

His clients' physical shortcomings could also lead to design innovations. In the early 1950s Balenciaga designed a collar "taken away from the neck and made to rest softly just about an inch away, allowing women and their pearls to breathe," as Guinness explained.[44] The detail was developed to disguise the short neck of *Harper's Bazaar* editor Carmel Snow.[45] *Vogue* fashion editor Susan Train remembers the Balenciaga wearer's seductive gesture of constantly shrugging a suit jacket or coat so that the collar fell backward like a geisha's kimono.[46] "Sleeves were shortened to uncover a wrist that permitted hands and bracelets to move," wrote Guinness, an effect that also attenuated the line of the arm.[47]

Balenciaga made the slips of his dresses to fit the body like a second skin but the garments fractionally larger. When the wearer moved, a current of air circulated between the layers, causing the dress alternately to float and caress the body, thus adding an element of mystery that blurred the reality of the figure beneath.[48] A similar effect was created by a waist seam that arced gently upward from the natural waistline in front and swooped subtly down beneath it in back. His fitters reassured clients that "Monsieur Balenciaga *likes* a little stomach," as Pauline de Rothschild relates in her "Appreciation" (reproduced on pages 7-12 of this volume). The structure of Balenciaga's clothes was often more important than what lay beneath, conferring "a dignity that could make up for any that might be lacking in a stocky dowager with a pouter-pigeon chest," as Kennedy Fraser has remarked.[49] "The stress of age was translated by the master into an elegant line."[50]

For Balenciaga, the greatest disgrace was to be *cursi*—vulgar.[51] He would often remark that you could put the same dress on two clients, and one would have chic and the other not.[52] His clothes demanded a certain carriage and hauteur on the part of the wearer, which his mannequins were encouraged to cultivate. "He was an individualist and worked for individualists," observed one journalist.[53] "You didn't feel that you needed to be pretty to wear Balenciaga," remembers Train. "You just had to stand up straight!"[54] "Balenciaga often said . . . women did not have to be perfect or even beautiful to wear his clothes," echoed the perfectly beautiful Guinness, a friend and patron of the designer's since the early 1940s, when they met in Madrid. "His clothes made them beautiful." She added, "One was a little afraid . . . of his clothes' being too difficult to wear. But they were not. They were so beautifully constructed, so perfectly thought out that there was not a woman in the world who could not wear them."[55] "If a woman came in a Balenciaga dress," noted Vreeland, "no other woman existed."[56]

As a result, Balenciaga's clients held him in reverence. Margaret Thompson Biddle, who habitually ordered favorite models in five or six different colorways, wrote in *Woman's Home Companion* of her relationship with the designer's work: "When I go to look at Balenciaga's collection as a customer, I am sometimes not quite sure that I want to wear some of his extreme models. But I have such faith in his taste that if I am certain a model is becoming I dare to order it. The first year I may be hesitant of wearing it, the second year I wear it and feel the height of fashion, and the third year the dress has become part of me."[57]

His clients' esteem also showed in their behavior. *WWD* noted, "Customers have such respect for the house that it never occurs to them not to pay their bills immediately (Balenciaga books are unique in couture annals for having practically no outstanding bills) or to come late for fittings."[58] When Snow introduced Loos and actress Paulette Goddard to Balenciaga at Le Grand Véfour, the storied Parisian restaurant, they both instinctively curtsied to him.[59]

As Rothschild recounts, Balenciaga absorbed lessons in Belle Époque elegance from the Proustian Marquesa de Casa Torres.[60] The marquesa's influence, however, was leavened with a more liberated and modern attitude that Balenciaga had witnessed in the singular person of Coco Chanel. Balenciaga had admired Chanel's boutique in the French resort of Biarritz (an hour's drive from San Sebastián) and had the opportunity to study her unique allure from afar when she played the baccarat tables at the celebrated casino in San Sebastián. At the time Balenciaga persuaded a wary Jesuit priest to effect an introduction, which he did with dire warnings about her reputation as a woman of flexible morals.[61] Later, Balenciaga bought Chanel models to copy and adapt in his Spanish establishments, admiring her for

8
House photograph of suit of black wool and bonnet of black silk organza, winter 1951

9
José Ortiz-Echagüe
Salamanca—Armuñesas in Sobinas, early 20th century

taking "all the chi-chi and fuss out of women's clothes."[62] In 1938 *Harper's Bazaar* noted of the *maison* Balenciaga, "This Spanish house abides by the great rule that elimination is the secret of chic," recalling Chanel's dictum that the truly elegant woman should appraise herself before leaving the house and remove one element of clothing or embellishment.[63] Balenciaga continued to use Chanel-branded fabrics during the 1940s, when her own fashion house was in hiatus, and the two designers remained intimate friends—Chanel offering Balenciaga extravagant gifts, including rock-crystal bibelots and her 1942 portrait by A. M. Cassandre—until a falling-out in the mid-1960s.[64]

On matters of design and philosophy, however, their approaches remained similar. As Colin McDowell has remarked, Balenciaga, like Chanel, "realized that women of fashion like to look exceptional but not outrageous: they wish their clothes to transform but not transmogrify their appearance."[65] Ballard also compared Balenciaga's fashion philosophy to that of Chanel. She commented, "He likes to make clothes in which women are comfortable, in which they can move their legs, and which they can put on with a minimum of effort."[66] As Balenciaga himself said, "When a woman walks the dress must walk, when she dances, the dress must dance, when she raises her arm the jacket should move discreetly."[67] "He was the son of a fisherman," observed Bunny Mellon. "His clothes, even the most sophisticated, reflected the simplicity and ease of movement."[68]

Balenciaga's extraordinary work ethic was inculcated through a hardscrabble childhood in the medieval town of Guetaria, situated in the Basque province of Guipúzcoa, on Spain's harsh and often unforgiving Atlantic coast, where he was born on January 21, 1895. His "Basque temperament—austere, independent, hardworking, determined, humourless"[69]—shaped the public face that he presented. (However, intimate friends and family have suggested a streak of dry humor that might have been revealed in private.) Guetaria was a fishing town that had raised adventurers and explorers keen to travel beyond its horizons, as Balenciaga himself would. Its native son Juan Sebastián Elcano completed the first circumnavigation of the globe in 1522, taking over Ferdinand Magellan's mission that set out in 1519.

Balenciaga's father, José Balenciaga Basurto, was a sailor who became a *patrón de escampavía*, the captain of a rowboat called *Guipuzcoana* that ferried people between the port and their larger crafts, including Alfonso XIII and his British-born queen, Victoria Eugenia (popularly known as Queen Ena), whom he would transport from the port or Miramar Palace to the royal yacht.[70] He eventually rose to a position of some prominence in the village and for a period became its mayor.[71] Nonetheless, the Balenciaga family was of modest means. They occupied the lower floors of 12, calle Aldamar, a humble establishment of flint stone and plaster in one of the four narrow streets that constitute Guetaria's old town.[72] Those crowded streets provide an almost theatrically framed perspective of the imposing nineteenth-century redbrick villa, with its geometric blue tile trim and pretty fretwork balconies, on the hill that rises above the village and that was the summer home of the Marqués de

Casa Torres.[73] The young Balenciaga was apparently captivated by the elegance of the marquesa and by the gowns from the great Parisian couturiers that his mother, a seamstress, helped her to unpack.[74] The vision of this woman and the world that she represented influenced his approach to fashion and his standard of elegance throughout his career.

José Balenciaga died in 1906 of a cerebral hemorrhage, and his widow, Martina Eizaguirre Embil, became a jobbing seamstress to support her family—Cristóbal, his sister, Maria Augustina, and his younger brother, Juan Martín.[75] A beloved figure in the village, Doña Martina also helped in community tasks, mending fishing nets and even helping as a midwife.[76] Cristóbal was devoted to her. He later preserved his mother's sewing machine as an almost religious relic, displaying it in his farmhouse at Monte Igueldo, overlooking La Concha, the corniche of San Sebastián.[77] Although the majority of men in Guetaria's tiny population of around thirteen hundred in 1897[78] harvested the land or sea for a living, Balenciaga the altar boy considered the church as a career.[79] The fourteenth-century Church of San Salvador, which dominates the village, was already a tourist destination by the turn of the century.[80] But at the age of six Balenciaga, presumably inspired by his mother's example, cut his first coat—for his cat. "But the cat kept moving, and Balenciaga became more and more frustrated," as Givenchy has related. "That could have been his first lesson in making clothes for people who moved."[81] This lesson learned, Balenciaga was more engaged by his mother's world than by the prospect of following either his uncle into the church or his father into a life at sea.

Martina Eizaguirre's work took her into the homes of some of the local aristocrats who had followed the example of Alfonso XIII, whose residence, Miramar Palace, had made nearby San Sebastián, "the Pearl of the Cantabrian Sea," into a fashionable summer resort.[82] As Rothschild notes, Balenciaga's first foray into the world of the haute couture was when he was emboldened to ask if he might copy one of the Marquesa de Casa Torres's Parisian suits (friends of Balenciaga's who have related the story ascribe the suit variously to Drécoll, Redfern, or Paul Poiret). Amused by this request from a child on the cusp of his teens, she indulged him and was pleased enough with the result to wear it.

The marquesa lifted the curtain on the world of the Parisian couture—the extravagant *tenues* created by the Belle Époque houses of Charles Frederick Worth, Jacques Doucet, Redfern, and Drécoll—and nurtured his career.[83] According to Rothschild, the magnificent hats of the era (often created by the great modiste Caroline Reboux, milliner to Empress Eugénie) were brought to dress fittings so that their proportions could be carefully calibrated to the ensembles with which they were intended to be worn.[84] The mannequins at those illustrious houses wore high-necked, long-sleeved, and close-fitting black jersey maillots beneath the garments they were presenting, so that their mortal flesh would not make contact with the fabrics intended for the clients. Similarly, in the 1960s Balenciaga's mannequins wore fitted black slips (embroidered with their names) during their fittings—a neutral base upon which he could

Tom Kublin
"Fishnet" coat in white velvet, made by Judith Barbier for Balenciaga;
evening dress of ivory satin with fuchsia satin belt, 1964
Originally published in *Harper's Bazaar*, November 1964

build his toiles. When Balenciaga introduced the revolutionary body stocking, which he showed under a cage of feathered chiffon, it was also dubbed the *maillot*—however, its purpose was to enhance and accentuate, rather than obfuscate, the body. "Everyone was going up in foam and thunder," recalled Vreeland of that heady moment. "We didn't know what we were *doing*, it was so glorious."[85]

Unlike many of his fellow Paris-based couturiers (Dior, Pierre Balmain, and Jacques Fath among them), whose backgrounds were bourgeois and whose educations were relatively extensive, Balenciaga (like Chanel) was largely self-taught and (unlike Chanel) remained surprisingly unworldly.[86] He left grammar school at the age of thirteen to learn a trade (at the tailoring establishment Casa Gómez) and earn a living to help support his family, eventually joining the Galerías El Louvre in San Sebastián, one of the city's several Francophile establishments.[87] At the time San Sebastián was "the rendezvous of Spanish society and of the 'beau monde' of Europe," and its style emporia "tempted with the latest Paris fashion and English sporting goods."[88] Perhaps taking its cue from the dandified monarch, the city was a center for English masculine tailoring—fashion historian Lesley Miller has described it as the hub of "Spanish Brummelism"—whose principles and craft Balenciaga admired and learned.[89] The earliest extant Balenciaga garment is the going-away outfit he made for his cousin Salvadora Egaña Balenciaga's wedding in 1912, when he was just seventeen.[90] A suit of figured black silk with an ivory lace jabot, it combines the austere with the fanciful in what came to be recognized as Balenciaga's trademark manner. As *Vogue* observed in 1963, "Balenciaga combines with drama—for which he has a Spaniard's quick sensitivity—a worldly sense of discretion."[91]

At the age of nineteen Balenciaga opened his own dressmaking establishment in San Sebastián, quietly echoing the pattern of the Parisian couturiers who followed their clients to the fashionable French watering holes and set up shop, providing not only garments appropriate to casino life and evening entertainment but also the *sportif* clothing created for the newly emerging culture of sun worship and beach activity. By the mid-1920s Chanel and Jean Patou had salons and boutiques in Deauville and Biarritz, and Captain Edward Molyneux had a branch in Cannes. Like Chanel, Balenciaga expanded from a resort city to the national capital and beyond, opening salons in Madrid and Barcelona. At these establishments, in addition to offering his own designs, Balenciaga greatly enhanced his knowledge of his craft by buying clothes from the Parisian couturiers he admired and then adapting their designs for his Spanish clientele.[92] The creators for whom he had a special empathy included Chanel and the great Madeleine Vionnet, who transformed the construction and fit of women's clothes with her mastery of the bias cut—an effect achieved by the women of turn-of-the-century Seville when they folded their *mantóns de Manila* (embroidered silk shawls) diagonally and took advantage of the resulting elasticity to drape them close to the bodice. Vionnet later recalled that when Balenciaga visited her salon in the early 1930s she questioned his need to acquire her models to copy in his Spanish salons, feeling that his own designs were

already accomplished enough. "Your clothes, Madame, inspire me," he answered.[93]

Vionnet remained a friend, and Balenciaga dressed her in the 1960s, as he did Elsa Schiaparelli, whose clothes he had also bought in the 1930s, during her heyday.[94] Schiaparelli paid him the ultimate compliment when she said that Balenciaga was the only couturier to dare to do what he liked, a surprising homage from a designer who built her career on audacity.[95] Balenciaga also admired Madeleine Chéruit—"who asserted not so much of a style as a certain piquancy and suppleness that made for chic," as Cecil Beaton expressed it[96]—as well as Augustabernard and Louiseboulanger, who were known for subtle sophistication and innovative cutting and draping techniques. For a period in the 1920s Balenciaga even elided his first and last names as these couturieres had done.[97]

The ranks of Balenciaga's clients soon swelled to include the Spanish royal family. By the age of twenty-one Balenciaga was dressing Queen Marie Christine, Infanta Isabel Alfonsa, and Queen Ena, who indulged her interest in fashion in the face of strong disapproval from the straitlaced *beatas* (meddlesome, self-righteous women) in her husband's court, which was then considered the most hidebound in Europe.[98] According to Feliza Salvagnac, the head of the couturier's *flou*, or dressmaking workroom, the queen "thought Balenciaga was the greatest man in fashion that ever existed."[99]

On April 14, 1931, the Second Republic was declared, and Alfonso XIII was exiled by the government. The ensuing upheavals and the temporary loss of Balenciaga's essential clientele effectively shuttered his businesses, resulting in bankruptcy.[100] As Spanish law forbade the use of a name associated with bankruptcy, when he reopened his house in San Sebastián, followed by those in Madrid and Barcelona, it was under the name Eisa, a diminution of his mother's maiden name, Eizaguirre.[101] Balenciaga's beloved sister Maria Augustina, his niece Tina, and his nephew José operated these establishments.[102]

The Spanish Civil War (which began with Franco's call to arms on July 18, 1936, and ended on April 1, 1939, when the last of the Republican forces fell to Nationalist troops supported by Fascist Italy and Nazi Germany) forced Balenciaga into exile. He went first to London. He was an admirer of British tailoring, and the capital's tradition of court dressmaking for a demanding, patrician clientele closely paralleled Balenciaga's own experience. He approached the couturier Norman Hartnell, but neither Hartnell nor the department store Selfridges could help him; the issue of a work visa may also have presented problems.[103] Thus Balenciaga turned his sights instead on Paris, probably at the urging of his intimate friend Vladzio Zawrorowski d'Attainville, a glamorous Franco-Russian architect and decorator whose elegant mother lived there. Balenciaga's significant relationship with the aristocratic d'Attainville, whom he seems to have met in the 1920s, burnished his taste and brought about a discreet social metamorphosis.[104]

On the modest capital of one hundred thousand francs, provided by d'Attainville and a fellow émigré, Nicolas Bizcarrondo (whom Balenciaga had apparently met in an air-raid shelter in San Sebastián), Balenciaga established his couture house.[105] He chose the fourth floor of an imposing 1887 apartment building at 10, avenue Georges V, next to the house of the Chicago-born couturier Main Bocher.[106] The decor, with white walls and baroque scrolled moldings, resembled a stage set. The boutique that he opened in 1948, designed by Christos Bellos, had exquisite display windows decorated by the sculptor Janine Janet that "never showed anything as vulgar as garments," instead featuring "the best gloves in Paris" (by Givenchy), scarves (often designed by Sache), and the house fragrances, Le Dix and Quadrille.[107]

The atmosphere throughout the building was serious and even forbidding. André Courrèges noted that the all-white studio was "unornamented and intensely silent" unless someone made the fatal mistake of handing Balenciaga a pencil instead of scissors, say, and his rare temper shook the house.[108] In contrast to the frenetic buzz of activity of a house like Balmain's, with its lively *directrice* Ginette Spanier (a friend of luminaries in the entertainment world, including Noël Coward and Marlene Dietrich), or Dior's (where Suzanne Luling held court), the atmosphere at the house of Balenciaga was "extremely severe," recalls client Rosamond Bernier. The formidable *directrice*, Renée Tamisier, known by the courtesy title Madame Renée, was "like the superior of a very good convent."[109] "It was reverential, with an absolute cathedral-like silence," according to Deeda Blair. "Going to a Balenciaga collection was like going to church," said Seventh Avenue designer Jerry Silverman.[110]

It was no mean feat to penetrate the inner sanctum, past "his twin dragons," Madame Renée and the Russian-born *vendeuse* Madame Véra, who guarded the entrance to the salon and vetted visitors from a Louis XV desk. "It was a little like an audience with the pope," according to an American store buyer. When one client dared to ask if she might bring a friend to a showing, Madame Renée answered, "Balenciaga does not indulge curious women." And when a preeminent store buyer asked if he could bring the wife of a prominent movie director to a showing, Madame Renée insisted that she bring a passport to confirm her identity.[111]

"Balenciaga would not allow any of his staff to smile so that their teeth showed," Percy Savage recalled. "He thought it vulgar."[112] Balenciaga's house mannequins contributed to the austere atmosphere. Unlike the celebrated *cabines* of fetching and occasionally high-profile beauties at the houses of Dior, Balmain, and Fath—or the patrician *cabine* chez Chanel, whose mannequins were all ruthlessly made over in the designer's own image—Balenciaga's mannequins were chosen for how they reflected the different body types of his clients rather than for conventional allure. They received a payment each time an outfit made for and shown by them was sold. "The greatest monster of them all, Colette," noted Ballard, "sold more costumes than any other girl has sold for him, walking with her Dracula walk, her big head low like a bull ready to charge, her shoulders hunched

down, her arms swinging low, and a look of almost violent hatred on her face as she passed, concealing the number of the dress from the spectators."[113] Balenciaga instructed his mannequins in the walk that he preferred: a swift and determined gait with a hint of a spring in the step—very different from the rapid half turns favored at other couture houses.[114] Bernier, who first visited in 1946, remembers the Balenciaga *cabine* being "unbelievably plain, some of them distractingly wool-eyed. . . . The master said that the girls were never to smile, never to look at the public, at the people, but to look over their heads. So they strode in silence."[115] Balenciaga was fond of quoting Salvador Dalí: "A distinguished lady always has a disagreeable air."[116]

Balenciaga prepared his debut collection, for winter 1937, as the civil war reached new heights of violence that included the firebombing of Basque towns. He was praised for his artfully cut little black dresses, their sobriety relieved by a flattering twist of pearls at the neck—a Spanish trope. (Franco's wife, María del Carmen Polo-Vereterra y Martínez-Valdés, was known as Doña Collares for her preference for pearl necklaces.)[117] "Perhaps it's the threat of war in Europe, perhaps it's the fear of looking too rich for the rabble," speculated *Harper's Bazaar* of these austere creations, noting that "the black is so black it hits you like a blow. . . . Thick Spanish black, almost velvety, a night without stars, which makes the ordinary black seem almost gray."[118]

"No one has ever entered Paris and completely taken over French dressmaking as this strong Spaniard did with his strong, scrupulous shapes," remembered Vreeland, then a fashion editor at *Harper's Bazaar*, of Balenciaga's 1937 Parisian debut.[119] It was Vreeland's editor, the prescient and powerful Snow, who truly recognized Balenciaga's genius at the time. "For myself a great light burst on the fashion world when I saw the first Paris collection of Cristóbal Balenciaga," Snow recalled. "My first glimpse of the severe elegance of his clothes made me eager to follow his development. His very individual style was too new, too different, to be widely appreciated on its first appearance. . . . But I somehow knew (Irish divination?) that this designer would revolutionize fashion."[120]

Balenciaga, of course, brought with him an established Spanish clientele—many of whom, like himself, were exiles and could not have failed to respond to the potent memories of their homeland embedded in his designs. A radio reviewer praised "an enchanting collection as heady as a Spanish wine."[121] And *Harper's Bazaar* noted colors that were "rather Spanish-dark, in unusual combinations, like mustard on deepest raspberry and dull green on prune."[122]

But the striking elegance of Balenciaga's clothes and the powerful press coverage that documented them immediately attracted an international clientele as well. Leaders of fashion such as the Duchess of Windsor, Mrs. Rodman de Heeren, Helena Rubinstein, Clare Boothe Luce, and the Honorable Daisy Fellowes became clients. By 1938, in the second year of his business, publications including *Vogue*, *Harper's Bazaar*, and *L'Officiel* gave Balenciaga's work equal weight to that of the established fashion houses in Paris. By 1940 *Harper's Bazaar* could make the extraordinary claim that "almost every woman, directly or indirectly, has worn a Balenciaga."[123]

Yet little was known of the man himself. Between establishing his fashion house and producing his collections, Balenciaga simply had no time to meet the press and clients. The language barrier—he was fluent only in Spanish—was another impediment. As a result, the urbane d'Attainville became the de facto public face of the house. His role was "to direct the shop and meet the world for him," as *Harper's Bazaar* noted.[124] It was not until February 1940, when d'Attainville was called up for military service, that Balenciaga was forced to interact with clients. In addition to his larger role, after 1942 d'Attainville replaced the fashionable Legroux sisters as the house milliner, creating the antic headdresses that were the single element of fantasy in which Balenciaga indulged.[125]

D'Attainville shrewdly realized the publicity value generated by the unusual strategy of having the designer be a figure of mystery. Helena Rubinstein knew Balenciaga as "the Spaniard That Nobody Ever Sees."[126] "True to his appearance," remarked Beaton, "the great dressmaker avoids publicity and the attentions and claims of worldly women."[127] Anny Latour observed, "The atmosphere of mystery which surrounds this Spanish individualist, the icy coldness with which every journalist is received, whether intentional or not, are just as effective as the loud beating of advertising drums."[128]

Balenciaga meanwhile controlled every aspect of the creative process, sketching ideas himself or developing them with a close band of associates.[129] The extant studio sketches, when matched to the finished garments—which were documented photographically for copyright purposes and rendered once more in their completed form for the benefit of the clients and buyers—reveal the tremendous development that took place between the idea and the realization of the garment, a testament to Balenciaga's organic approach during his intense fitting sessions. "The sketch is only the beginning of the design," he told his client Margaret Biddle. "I must think it all through from the fabric to the shoes until I see the woman all complete as in a colored photograph."[130]

After Germany invaded Poland on September 1, 1939, Balenciaga's world changed once more. German forces occupied Paris on June 22, 1940, by which time the British-born Molyneux and the American Main Bocher (whose salon, adjacent to his own, Balenciaga later acquired) had fled France for London and New York, respectively. The Italian-born Schiaparelli had embarked on a successful lecture tour of America, defying her country by raising funds for the Allied cause. (Schiaparelli's salon continued to operate during the occupation, under the supervision of her *directrice*.) Although Franco's Spain declared itself "nonbelligerent," the Fascist country was an ideological ally of the Axis powers, and as a result Balenciaga's position in Paris was relatively favored in the eyes of the occupiers. The Germans made repeated attempts to relocate the Paris haute couture establishment to Berlin, but Lucien Lelong, the head of the Chambre Syndicale de la Couture, the industry's official organizing body, strenuously resisted this move.[131] "Hitler wanted to transfer the French couture to Berlin," Balenciaga recalled. "He sent six enormous Germans to see me—much taller than I—to talk about it. I said that he might just as well take all the bulls to Berlin and try and train the bullfighters there."[132]

Apparently exasperated by Lelong's persuasive resistance, in 1944 the Germans closed the houses of both Balenciaga and Madame Grès on the grounds that they had flouted the strict new rules pertaining to fabric usage. Only through the intervention of the Spanish ambassador was Balenciaga eventually allowed to reopen. Grès had to renounce her signature draped-jersey dresses, which used extravagant lengths of fabric that were specially woven to triple width, before she was permitted to present her collections once more.[133]

Throughout the war Balenciaga generally resisted the extreme fashions concocted by many other couture houses for the parvenu black marketers, known as *BOF* (for the *beurre, oeufs,* and *fromage* that they traded at exorbitant prices), who demanded flamboyant effects for their cash.[134] During the occupation, some news of Balenciaga's fashions percolated to America through his salons in Barcelona and Madrid. Gloria Guinness claimed, "More Balenciaga dresses were smuggled out of Paris than any other French item, including perfume."[135] For American *Vogue's* July 1941 issue, Eric (Carl Erickson) sketched a trio of tailored suits that were made at Eisa in Barcelona and exported to America, where they were retailed by a specialty salon and copied by Henri Bendel. By March 1944, when *Harper's Bazaar* photographed the actress Leonora Corbett in one of the "huge . . . elegant, outrageous hats" (presumably designed by d'Attainville) from Balenciaga's Madrid salon, the magazine's tone was more acerbic. "Colossal concoctions like these are worn with dresses made from silks woven by French mills which the Nazis permit to operate for the luxury trade," reported the magazine, noting that the designer "is doing flourishing business in Madrid, Barcelona, San Sebastián, and Paris. . . . [The hats] are seen at Maxim's in Paris and at the Ritz in Madrid, wherever food and wine are flowing just around the corner from starvation, they're worn on heads that do not seem to lie uneasy—Marie-Antoinette once wore a frigate in her hair."[136]

However, Balenciaga limited his extravagances to his head wear. Meanwhile, he continued to refine and perfect the fashion silhouettes that he had initiated in the late 1930s. He drew on elements of Spanish regional dress that he had observed in his travels around the country and in his extensive library of fashion- and costume-related material. The peplum, for example, which was derived from the seventeenth-century court bodice, engaged him for decades. In response to wartime fabric restrictions and the need for clothes with multiple functions, practical, layered garments and accessories that could be transformed easily were called into service.

After the liberation on August 25, 1944, returning international journalists and clients were impressed by the quiet assurance of Balenciaga's clothes, embodied by the supremely elegant

Harper's BAZAAR

November 1952

Incorporating Junior Bazaar

Fashion
Southbound
Lingerie and Fur—
The Present News

The Boy Who Ran Away

by Charles Jackson

60 cents

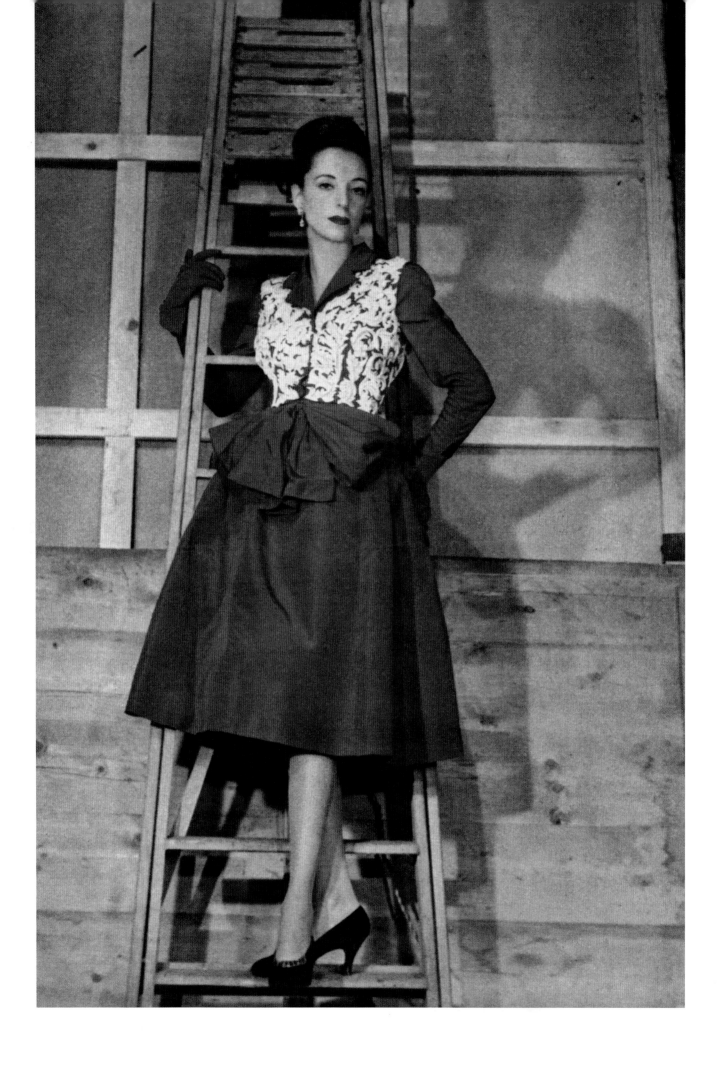

Gloria Rubio (later Guinness), who was much photographed in her Balenciaga wardrobe (see pl. 12). Balenciaga's silhouette of the period, with the bodice closely following the line of the body and a gentle fullness to the hips, remained essentially unchanged from the late 1930s; he told *Harper's Bazaar* that there would be "no radical change in fashion until this transition [postwar] period is over and our way of life established."[137] On February 12, 1947, however, Christian Dior, already celebrated by fashion insiders for his work at the house of Lucien Lelong, launched his own *maison de couture* (with the considerable financial backing of textile magnate Marcel Boussac).[138] His Ligne Corolle, dubbed the "New Look" by Snow, was a sensational success. It was not a radical departure from the line that Balenciaga was promoting. However, Balenciaga's silhouettes were achieved through cut and the manipulation of the intrinsic properties of the fabrics, whereas Dior's designs depended on elaborate underpinnings. Balenciaga's clothes "skimmed the body but were never tight," remembers Susan Train. "You were never strangled into them, whereas Dior had a great deal of interior construction."[139] Balenciaga would have been appalled by Nancy Mitford's rapturous description of a Dior suit that she ordered in the spring of 1948: "The skirt has sort of stays at which one tugs until giddiness intervenes—the basque of the coat stuck out with whalebone."[140] "My husband once asked [Balenciaga] to come to his rescue in doing up a Dior dress with thirty tiny buttons up the back," recalled Ballard, "and Balenciaga kept muttering as he buttoned, 'But Christian is mad, mad!'"[141]

A year after Dior's debut, d'Attainville died unexpectedly. Balenciaga was so distraught that he contemplated closing his business. As a freelance fashion-sketch artist in the late 1930s, Dior had sold designs to Balenciaga, and he revered his talent.[142] Alarmed at the prospect of "such a huge loss of the prestige of Paris couture," Dior persuaded Balmain to join him on a visit to Balenciaga to dissuade him from this course. The pair arrived at the studio bearing the gift of a Braque drawing.[143] Dior's generosity continued. In July 1949, when strikes threatened the operation of Balenciaga's couture workrooms, Dior and his business director, Jacques Rouët, went to offer the Dior seamstresses—who were not members of the Chambre Syndicale's striking union—to help finish his collection. Balenciaga was touched but declined the offer.[144]

Dior's profound respect for Balenciaga's work was not reciprocated. They could not have been more different. For Ernestine Carter, "Dior was like Mozart, a bubbling fountain of seemingly endless happy inspiration; Balenciaga, like Granados's *Goyescas*, somber, brooding, dignified."[145] Ballard explained that Balenciaga "never understood about Dior, his genius for publicity or his great fame. His own hatred for the press was augmented by their slavish devotion to everything Dior did."[146] "He abhorred publicity and fame," wrote Dior. "But no one deserved it more."[147] "Balenciaga is *the* success of the season," commented *Harper's Bazaar* of the winter 1950 collection. "After his opening there was a five minute ovation, but the 'monk of the couture' still refused to appear."[148]

Balenciaga was also profoundly disillusioned by his fickle clients, who flocked to Dior to acquire the latest look. This, as he related to Givenchy, strengthened his resolve to remove himself further still from personal interaction with them or even to accept their plaudits after his collections.[149] Ballard once asked Balenciaga to escort her to a garden party at the extravagant Louis XVI-revival *hôtel* in Neuilly of the best-dressed society ornament Patricia Lopez-Willshaw. There, Balenciaga was "horrified by the way society women looked en masse" and appalled by the clothes created by his fellow couturiers.[150]

The shy and retiring Balenciaga lived, as his friend Guinness related, "in a world of 'dreamed beauty,' a world of elegance and dignity and quiet luxury."[151] As Beaton observed, "It took many years of hard work to compensate for his background, his early lack of opportunities and education."[152] Balenciaga's appreciation of Spanish art seems to have been instinctive. Ballard claimed, for instance, that he resisted her efforts to get him to join her on visits to the Prado, although its iconic works find endless echoes in his creations.[153] He traveled little; he made three brief visits to New York (where he was intimidated by the inhuman scale of the high-rises) and one sightseeing trip to Italy with Bizcarrondo ("[The Bizcarrondos] were knowledgeable, cultivated people who introduced him to the treasures of Italy, which left Balenciaga impressed but a little intimidated"). In Paris he dined with intimates at the Café Allard, a bistro on the Left Bank.[154] He visited the spa at Fitero in Navarra; skied in Saint Moritz, Arosa, and Davos; and retreated after his collections to his austerely appointed seventeenth-century farmhouse at Monte Igueldo.

"He had worked very hard since he was a child, and there had never been time for casual relationships or superficialities," noted Ballard. "He was capable only of intimate friendship, the kind that had no complicated social machinery to keep oiled."[155] Balenciaga was also socially constrained in Paris by his limited language skills, although Snow claimed, "Ours is an intuitive relationship that simply ignores the language barrier—I speak no Spanish, he speaks no English, our French isn't especially competent—but I never once doubted that I could understand all he was saying."[156] Balenciaga communicated in Spanish with his close-knit team of design associates. The pattern of his life was essentially determined by the intense routine of creating the Paris collections and supervising his Spanish couture houses. For Balenciaga, who sketched ideas during sleepless nights, the garment essentially began not with a sketch but with the fabric.[157]

The French government provided subsidies to Parisian fashion houses as long as they limited their use of foreign fabrics to 10 percent. Balenciaga forwent these financial incentives. Instead, he developed close working relationships and in some cases friendships with, among others, Gustave Zumsteg at Abraham in Zurich, with whom he eventually developed gazar, the stiff, loosely woven silk gauze that enabled him to tailor evening gowns as crisply as his suits and coats and resulted in some of his most remarkably architectural garments; and Britain's Miki Ascher and Bernat Klein, who worked on

12
Cecil Beaton
Gloria Guinness wearing dinner dress of red taffeta with baroque-embroidered waistcoat
Originally published in *Vogue*, December 15, 1945

extraordinary textural woolens. He also sourced fabric from mills in Scotland, Lancashire, and Italy. Balenciaga's fabric combinations, too, were often startling but effective: a fall of flaxen slipper satin on a sheath of black wool crepe, perhaps, or a draped gown of silver duchesse satin designed to be worn under a coat of silver lamé, its texture woven to simulate armorial braided chains.

Once the fabric selections were made, the true work began. Feliza Salvagnac, who was brought from San Sebastián to Paris in 1937 and headed Balenciaga's dressmaking workroom until he closed the house, recalled that he "could easily have ninety fittings for a single collection. You needed courage to work with him; Balenciaga's hypercritical eye saw every flaw. But you knew that every correction was justified, so you accepted it."[158] In each of the ninety-three collections of Balenciaga's career, there was always one black dress that was entirely cut and made by him.[159]

The Paris collections often included more than two hundred models, shown in presentations that lasted as long as two hours. For the Eisa salons a selection was made of those models considered most suitable for the Spanish market, and the Paris staff would travel with their toiles to explain the finer points of the new clothes. There Balenciaga dressed "a slightly staider and more frugal clientele" (Señora Franco brought her own discount fabrics to be made up).[160] The Eisa outposts were also a boon to visiting Americans because Balenciaga clothes could be acquired there "for a fraction of the price."[161] "The clothes are superb and quite a bit cheaper than in Paris," remarked Cordelia Biddle Robertson.[162] And, as Régine d'Estribaud has noted, the benefit extended "to French women too."[163] Franco's protectionist policies meant that it was illegal to import textiles into Spain, whose own thriving textile industry was centered largely around Barcelona. As a result, stylish women gravitated to Eisa to purchase Balenciaga's clothes made in less expensive Spanish fabrics. Balenciaga also used these outposts to train or hone his technicians, allowing them to learn from their mistakes before they went to Paris, where mistakes were not indulged. Courrèges and Emanuel Ungaro, who began their careers as tailors for Balenciaga, both worked at Eisa.[164]

Favored clients—from the wealthy Claudia Heard de Osborne to the "poor as a church mouse" Rosamond Bernier (as she described herself)—were often given the references for the fabrics of the original Paris models so that they could acquire them and discreetly provide them to their Eisa fitters. (The smuggling of textiles across the border was a long-established tradition.) For instance, Bernier—who was favored by Madame Renée for her distinguished appearance, her command of Spanish, and her connections to the contemporary art world (and especially to Picasso)—was given the fabric references for six models that she admired in a mid-century collection and had them made up at Eisa in Madrid. When she returned to Paris wearing these clothes, however, a disdainful Madame Renée told her "they don't even know how to fit there" and had them all refitted in Paris at no charge.[165]

Intimate friends whose fittings Balenciaga did deign to supervise might have been given cause to regret the intervention. As Salvagnac recalled, "We worked all night before every opening. Many times he changed the designs the day before the collection opened, tore the clothes apart as they didn't seem perfect enough for him."[166]

Balenciaga shared with Chanel an obsession with the set of a sleeve. "Working sometimes on the cut of a sleeve," noted Guinness, "he would neglect all else and go without food or sleep for days and nights."[167] Sonsoles Díez de Rivera, daughter of the Marquesa de Llanzol, remembers, "His great obsession was the sleeves and how they fitted." She often found herself, like many others, having to leave Balenciaga's salons in a borrowed garment because he had taken her own to rework a sleeve he considered badly done.[168] After endless fittings with Balenciaga in Madrid, during which he insisted the tailor Juan reset the sleeves again and again, Ballard finally hid the newly delivered suit under a voluminous coat, realizing that she would never leave with it otherwise. She remarked that Balenciaga was "as jealously ambitious for a suit of his as a mother for the career of her only son."[169]

Balenciaga's perfectionism extended to his highly refined color sense, "sharpened to such a remarkable degree," noted Beaton, "that he can unerringly scan four hundred colors and choose the right one for his purpose."[170] "You've never seen such colors," enthused Vreeland, "you've never seen such violets! My God, pink violets, blue violets! Suddenly you were in a nunnery, you were in a monastery."[171] Clients were generally dissuaded from altering the essential concept of the garment as Balenciaga had created it—especially by the 1950s, when he had achieved the authority to impose his will, through his *vendeuses*, in this area. However, there were instances when they could change the colors. By the 1960s Balenciaga occasionally sent out pairs of particularly innovative garments in contrasting colorways—or one in black, the other in a vibrant tone—for the sort of dramatic and even playful effect that is captured in Tom Kublin's films of the runway shows from 1961 through 1968.

A very good client like Elizabeth Parke Firestone, for instance, who would not wear black, was indulged when she ordered clothes that had been presented in that hue (often the statement pieces in the collection) in a gamut of blues, which she felt better complemented her golden hair and marshmallow complexion. Bunny Mellon was also drawn to a palette of sapphire blues. Balenciaga's color sense was recognized as exceptional, and only a brave and intransigent client—or an artist—would dare improve upon it. When Bernier visited Henri Matisse wearing Balenciaga's dramatic orange coat over a little black dress, the artist bade her to "'wear a yellow scarf with it.' And I did. And he was absolutely right."[172]

Balenciaga's bravura use of color reached beyond the world of fashion. In 1961, the fearless beauty magnate Helena Rubinstein (pl. 13), then eighty-nine, commissioned the young decorator David Hicks to decorate the drawing room of her London apartment on Hyde Park. When asked about a preferred color for the large drawing room, Rubinstein summoned an assistant to cut a section of the purple-violet linen from the inner hem of her Balenciaga suit. Hicks "pasted [it] in his scrapbook, where it remained like a religious relic."[173] The resulting interior, featuring an eclectic gathering of mid-nineteenth-century Belter chairs, African sculpture, and contemporary art set against walls matched to that vivid purple, heralded a whole new era of bold decoration, generated enormous publicity and interest, and sealed Hicks's reputation as the taste-making decorator of his era.

The house of Balenciaga was notable for its exceedingly high prices, but certain clients–whose youth and style Madame Renée deemed effective advertisements–were given special consideration. These included Catherine "Deeda" Gerlach (who wore an ice-blue aléoutienne evening dress and stole by Balenciaga for her 1961 wedding to William McCormick Blair, Jr.),[174] Doris Brynner (for whose husband, Yul, Balenciaga designed a jacket derived from that of a Basque fisherman),[175] and Bernier. Invited clients could also acquire the model garments at the sales held at the end of the season. "They simply closed off an area like a baseball players' bull pen, that is to say an enclave," remembers Bernier. "They were all hung up, and it was really help yourself. I remember seeing Marlene Dietrich desperately pulling something over her head. So that was sort of a funny thing, the communal dressing with these rather grand ladies, such as Marlene, fending for themselves."[176]

Although from the very beginning of his Paris career Balenciaga counted close friends among the ladies of the press–including *Vogue*'s Ballard (who was introduced to him by the worldly photographer André Durst months before he presented his first collection)[177] and *Harper's Bazaar*'s Snow and Marie-Louise Bousquet (through whom Balenciaga met Givenchy)–he nevertheless made life complicated for them. In March 1956, exasperated by the dissemination of his ideas through press coverage and the ensuing copying of his designs, Balenciaga (in tandem with Givenchy) announced that his press showings would be held a month after he had presented his collections to clients and buyers and they had placed (and even received) their orders.[178] This effectively meant that the press had to return to Paris en masse a month after they had seen and reported on the other couture shows. It also ensured that the two designers received independent coverage in a subsequent magazine issue, thus giving them the last, authoritative word.

In a rare interview granted in 1971 to Prudence Glynn of the London *Times*, Balenciaga, reflecting back on his career, provided some insight into his attitude toward the press. "This obsessive dislike of publicity is in no way caused by the feeling that he is too grand to bother," wrote Glynn. "It is caused, he told me passionately, by the absolute impossibility he finds of explaining his métier (the word he always uses) to anyone."[179] He famously pronounced that a couturier was required to be "an architect for perspective, a sculptor for form, a painter for color, a musician for harmony, and a philosopher for a sense of proportion."[180]

Balenciaga transferred the moral values by which he lived into his work. "The garment must not appear to have been manufactured, stretched, distorted," he told Givenchy, to whom he confided that he had never told a lie. "Everything must be natural, honest, and true."[181] Balenciaga's spirituality and integrity were also present in his general lack of materialism and his generosity toward others. Although he loved to shop in Rastro, Madrid's flea market, and piled up antique Cuenca rugs for apartments that were never ready to receive them, he was not acquisitive. He resolutely resisted lucrative licensing arrangements, unlike Dior, Fath, and other couturiers. "What would I buy?" he asked Ballard. "I have a car and too many houses."[182] Balenciaga was generous with his time and knowledge, as when he felt he had found a worthy acolyte (as he did in Givenchy), and also financially. In 1961 he gave Courrèges, then his tailor, the loan he had asked for to set up his own fashion house. When Courrèges had made the money to pay him back, Balenciaga refused to accept it.[183] Father Pieplu, the parish priest of Saint-Pierre de Chaillot, where Balenciaga regularly attended mass when he was in Paris, suggested that the designer had a higher purpose still, that his "clothes were supposed to reveal the deep harmony, beauty in its purest form; the reflection–beyond all distortions–of the Creator which everyone hides more or less in his inner self.

13
Graham Sutherland
Helena Rubinstein in a Red Brocade Balenciaga Gown, 1957, oil on canvas
Helena Rubinstein Foundation

M. Balenciaga in this way revealed and somehow remodeled the beauty of each individual."[184]

By the 1960s, although his influence was profound, Balenciaga, with his tight-knit circle of friends and acolytes and his punishing work schedule, was increasingly removed from contemporary developments. "Balenciaga did not concern himself with young–or rather, unmarried–women," Palmer White has noted. "His designing was rooted in an age-old, patrician Catholic society composed of a privileged few."[185] Yves Saint Laurent, then entering an era of irreverent and inventive design, felt that the influence of the essentially nineteenth-century style mores of the Marquesa de Casa Torres cast a long shadow and isolated Balenciaga from youth culture. Vreeland concurred that "Balenciaga wasn't interested in youth," although she acknowledged that "people would tell me fashion started in the streets, and I would always say I saw it first at Balenciaga."[186]

Yet, Balenciaga's summer 1968 collection, shown on the eve of Paris's student riots, was, as Pauline de Rothschild notes, "the collection of a very young man together with all the knowledge."[187] Balenciaga, then seventy-three, showed suits with tiny shorts (he had first shown culottes in 1939, hidden under wrap skirts), dresses miraculously fashioned from a single seam, and extraordinary trapezoid evening gowns created from gazar. But Balenciaga felt out of step in the face of fashion's dramatically shifting paradigm–from the couture for women of a certain age, substance, and worldly position to styles emerging from the street, inspired by a youthquake revolution that ushered in a pubescent body type. "This age is marked by the lack of elegance in women," he told Prudence Glynn in 1971. "The life which supported couture is finished. Real couture is a luxury which is just impossible to do anymore."[188]

"He knew how to streamline women of a certain age, those over forty," noted *WWD*. "In later years his clothes were too reserved, too studied, too middle-aging, and too constructed for young people."[189] Balenciaga's former mannequin Emmanuelle Khan, one of the earliest creators (with fellow *cabine* member Christiane Bailly) of fashion-forward ready-to-wear in Paris, railed against her former employer, accusing him of designing clothes that bore no relation to a woman's body. Lady Clare Rendlesham, the fashion editor of the youthquake British magazine *Queen*, ran a premature obituary of Balenciaga and Givenchy, declaring the demise of the haute couture.[190]

Although Balenciaga expressed an interest in exploring ready-to-wear ideas, as his protégés Courrèges and Ungaro had done, he also acknowledged (to the Marquesa de Llanzol, among others) that he felt it was too late for him to learn what was essentially a new métier. For instance, when he was commissioned in 1966 to design the new Air France uniforms, Balenciaga wanted to fit each of the six thousand uniforms himself.[191] "How could such a man have converted to 'ready-mades?'" asked Virginie Merlin-Teysserre in *Paris Match*.[192]

He was tired. As he later told Glynn, "When I was a young man I was told by a specialist that I could never pursue my chosen métier of couturier because I was far too delicate. Nobody knows what a hard métier it is. How killing is the work. Under all this luxury and glamour . . . *c'est la vie d'un chien* [it's a dog's life]!"[193] "At my age," as Merlin-Teysserre reported him saying, "you can change your life. You can't change your profession."[194]

And so, in May of 1968 he shut up shop. His four hundred "worshipful" employees first read about it in the newspapers.[195] Renée Tamisier signed their unapologetic termination letters.[196] His clients were also bereft. According to Vreeland, Mona Bismarck took to her bedroom for three days to mourn.[197] The considerable stock of unsold garments was sold for fifteen hundred francs apiece in a basement area that had been specially set up for the purpose.

Beyond the end of his career, the Balenciaga mystique endured. He was last seen in public on January 13, 1971, at the funeral mass for Chanel; his Christian forgiveness clearly trumped any lingering hurt he may have felt. He was coaxed out of retirement to create the dress for the marriage of María del Carmen Martínez-Bordiú y Franco, General Franco's granddaughter, to Alfonso de Bourbón y Dampierre, grandson of Alfonso XIII, in Madrid on March 9, 1972.[198] It would prove a stately coda to his career. Balenciaga had dressed her mother, María del Carmen Franco y Polo, as a Zurbarán Madonna; for the daughter he created a wedding dress (pl. 14) that evoked the glories of fifteenth-century Spanish court dress in its linear purity and restrained medieval embellishment. One of the most significant dresses of his career, it was also subject to his rigorous perfectionism. "Two days before [the wedding], he pulled the dress completely apart because he didn't like the way it fit," the bride recalled. "I thought I'd never get married."[199] It was a dress that might have been fashioned for Isabella I, queen of Castile and León, unifier of Spain, and supreme champion of the Catholic faith.

Balenciaga's bold plans for his retirement included finally touring the Spain whose mythic imagery and history had so resonated throughout his work but that he had barely been able to explore in the thirty years since he had established himself in Paris.[200] He traveled to Valencia with Ramón Esparza and Mitza Bricard, intending to buy a property near his friend the musician Rafael Calparsoro.[201] But on the return journey, on March 23, 1972, he suffered a fatal heart attack. Such was his intense discretion that even his close friend Givenchy knew nothing of his heart condition.[202] Balenciaga's body was taken back to Guetaria (Spanish law dictating burial within twenty-four hours),[203] and he was laid to rest beneath a gaunt block of glossy black granite in the town cemetery, "surrounded by fishermen and past sailors. The infinite Cantabrian Sea below."[204]

WWD headlined its story "The King Is Dead."[205]

14
Raymond de Larrain
Doña María del Carmen Martínez-Bordiú y Franco wearing wedding dress of embroidered white satin, 1972
Originally published in *Gaceta Illustrada*, March 19, 1972

15
Attributed to Francisco de Goya
Narcisa Barañana de Goicoechea, 1810, oil on canvas
The Metropolitan Museum of Art, New York, H. O. Havemeyer Collection,
bequest of Mrs. H. O. Havemeyer, 1929

SPANISH ART

"Balenciaga treated fabric like a sculptor treats clay or marble," wrote the German journalist Erica Billeter in 1970, "masterpieces, cut with scissors, sculpted in fabric, colored by an artist's fantasy."[1] Balenciaga's clients often had the same impression. Balenciaga, however, made no such case for himself as a fine artist, resolutely referring to his "métier."[2]

Vogue editor Bettina Ballard observed, surprisingly, that Balenciaga knew "little about his country or its art. I could never drag Cristóbal into the Prado with me."[3] However, Balenciaga's entire oeuvre resonates with echoes, loud or soft, of Spain's powerful art history. His personal art collection was eclectic, running the gamut from a seventeenth-century head of Christ by Francisco de Zurbarán to works by Georges Braque, his great friend the Basque sculptor Eduardo Chillida, and others.[4]

For his winter 1939 collection Balenciaga showed a group of evening gowns that were directly inspired by Diego Velázquez's celebrated 1650s portraits of Infanta Margarita and her ladies-in-waiting (see pls. 5, 30). These proved popular; *Vogue* and *Harper's Bazaar* published them, and Bergdorf Goodman bought the models. The timing was serendipitous. That summer Spain's newly installed Nationalist government consented to a planned exhibition of masterworks from the Prado and other institutions, including iconic paintings by El Greco, Bartolomé Esteban Murillo, Velázquez (thirty-four works), and Goya (thirty-eight) at the Musée d'Art et d'Histoire in Geneva.[5] Reinforcing Spain's significant cultural history and national identity, the pictures had a potent effect on the Parisian haute couture, and the press was quick to note the resonances in Balenciaga's work. "The new fashions are built in the romantic tradition, but the accent is on drama and not on dimples," wrote *Harper's Bazaar*. "Austerity and sumptuousness go hand in hand. . . . Direct from the exhibition of the Prado paintings in Geneva come dresses that are stiff and full like those in the Velázquez paintings; glycerined feather headdresses that follow the buttressed line of an [Infanta's] head; lots of dead, dramatic black lit by touches of vermilion."[6]

Velázquez's court portraits proved an enduring inspiration to Balenciaga. In his 1654 portrait of Infanta Margarita (pl. 29), Velázquez carefully described the scallop-edged black lace trim on her costume. Black lace, produced in Barcelona after it was introduced by the celebrated lace makers of Flanders—then under Spanish dominion—had been fashionable for a century.[7] Balenciaga used similar scallop-edged, black cotton lace to emphasize the lines of a white linen suit from summer 1948 (pl. 31). The trim outlining the hem of the jacket's broad peplum parallels the seventeenth-century court dressmaker's accentuation of the breadth of the infanta's *guardainfante*.

Balenciaga conceived stoles, trains, and fabric swaths—in which the unlined material (generally paper-silk taffeta or silk faille) falls as its inherent properties dictate—to provide textural and tonal contrast in his clothes. This painterly treatment also reflects the depiction of draperies in the works of El Greco and Zurbarán. As the Balenciaga scholar Marie-Andrée Jouve has observed, Balenciaga's straw-yellow satin stole that accompanies an austere black evening column from winter 1951 (pl. 19) echoes the yellow drapery in Zurbarán's *Annunciation* (1638–1639; pl. 20).[8] Another black wool evening sheath from summer 1950 features taupe silk-shantung bodice drapery that can be worn to hide or reveal the shoulders, its hip swath finishing in a train of entirely theatrical proportions (pl. 18). Jouve has also noted the oblique connection between the artful placement of the roses—painstakingly cut out from a printed

cotton textile and embroidered onto organza—in a Balenciaga dress from summer 1958 (pl. 27) and those scattered before the kneeling figure of Saint Francis in Zurbarán's *The Miracle of the Roses* (1630) (pl. 28).[9]

The pink taffeta that wraps the upper bodice of a summer 1951 embroidered ivory evening sheath is finished with a giant bow in back—although the wearer has the option to thread her arms through its loops as if sleeves (pl. 24). This bow reflects the extravagant volumes of looped fabric falling into trains depicted by Zurbarán in his portraits of Saint Elizabeth of Portugal and Saint Casilda of Toledo (pl. 23).

Zurbarán, the son of a haberdasher, was justly celebrated for his exquisitely rendered draperies; he apparently concocted their models on small-scale lay figures.[10] Flemish artists introduced to Spain the conceit of dressing female saints in elaborate contemporary court dress.[11] Zurbarán went farther still, inventing highly unusual combinations of color and pattern that hint at an exotic locale or an archaic costume, as befitting the portrayal of a long-dead saint such as the Muslim-born Casilda.

Unusual back treatments were a continual fascination for Balenciaga. Another was his interest in creating clothing that presented radically different silhouettes from different angles. According to fashion historian Aileen Ribeiro, Spanish women in Goya's era "were supposed to be as seductive from the back as from the front."[12] This influence reached an apotheosis of abstraction in Balenciaga's sculptural gazar dress of 1965 (pls. 25–26).

A soft-gray paper-silk taffeta dress in the collection of the Museum of the City of New York, resembling but not identical to the model shot by Clifford Coffin for *Vogue*'s November 1, 1948, issue (pl. 22), has a skirt that hangs plumb to the floor in front but sweeps into fullness in back. Remarkably, Balenciaga cut these elements from one piece, relying on the shifting grain of the fabric. The ateliers of most of his fellow couturiers would have required elaborate seaming and infrastructure to achieve this effect. For a satin evening dress of winter 1963 (pl. 21), Balenciaga manipulated the fabric from the back to the front, where, in another tour de force of subtle construction, its folds contrive a shapeliness to the bodice.

The hieratic court costume of Spain's golden age, depicted in magisterial portraits by artists such as Alonso Sánchez Coello, Sofonisba Anguissola, and Velázquez, informs many of Balenciaga's grander design statements, such as a magnificent 1950 evening dress, masterfully captured by Richard Avedon in his photograph of Dovima for *Harper's Bazaar* (pl. 78). In this example, Balenciaga softened the effect of the basque, or tight bodice, and farthingale worn by Infanta Margarita in Velázquez's *Las meninas* of 1656. The fashion had changed by 1666, when Juan Bautista Martínez del Mazo depicted her dressed in mourning for her father, Philip IV (pl. 202). Balenciaga modernized the idea by counterpointing the stiff basque with a ball-gown skirt fashioned from millefeuille layers of silk tulle, creating an ethereal effect. A superb sheath dress of winter 1950 in the collection of the Metropolitan Museum's Costume Institute, while following the conventional mid-century line, is lavished with embroidery by Métral of gold and silver braid, pearls, and beads that evokes the splendor of the jewels and richly embellished costumes worn by Infanta Isabella Clara Eugenia in her portraits by Sánchez Coello and Juan Pantoja de la Cruz from the last quarter of the sixteenth century. This dress was made for the same exacting client as the basque gown, the automotive heiress Thelma Chrysler Foy, whom the *New York Times* described as "the woman of the greatest taste . . . in New York."[13]

Balenciaga also responded to a softer age of extraordinary Spanish portraiture. "Goya, whether Balenciaga is aware of it or not, is always looking over his shoulder," wrote Ballard.[14] "He believes in lace and ribbon bows—never used in a fussy way but rather with true Spanish dignity."[15] Goya's dramatic portraits of the aristocratic women in the courts of Carlos III and Carlos IV—notably those of Cayetana de Silva, the flamboyant thirteenth Duchess of Alba—inspired Balenciaga throughout his career. And no wonder—"Detail for detail," as Robert Hughes has observed, "no great tragic artist has ever been more absorbed, in his untragic moments, by the minutiae of fashion than Goya."[16]

Goya's art captured a time of crisis in Spain, when the country was brought to its knees by economically devastating wars with France and England. At this time the *maja* and *majos* of the working class attempted to distinguish themselves from the pretentiously Francophile middle-class *petimetres* by adopting a style of dress that explicitly referenced aspects of uniquely Spanish regional costume, their attitude embodying a "sweetly truculent Spanishness."[17] Goya painted many of his sitters dressed in *maja* costume, including Queen Maria Luisa and the outrageously fashionable Duchess of Alba. Like the working class, the Spanish upper classes were keen to distance themselves from the merchant class and to reinforce a spirit of national identity. At times, even Goya himself dressed as a *majo*. "It was natural that he should adopt the air of a tough guy in the city," noted Hughes, "like a successful artist in 1960s New York wearing a black leather jacket."[18]

An exquisite black ball gown from Balenciaga's winter 1957 collection (pl. 33) is densely embroidered in a trellis of satin ribbons and tiny black silk fringe tassels that brings to mind both the fragile silk-gauze flowers of the Duchess of Alba's *basquina* in her 1797 portrait (pl. 32) and the net overskirt in a *maja* costume of ca. 1801 in the collection of the Museo del Traje in Madrid (pl. 46). The unusual yellow and black lace used in the skirts of a winter 1951 evening dress (pl. 45) suggests a similar palette. In her first Goya portrait of 1795 (pl. 44), the duchess is shown in a dotted white muslin dress, its simplicity evoking the infamously informal *gaulle* (muslin chemise) in which Elisabeth Louise Vigée-LeBrun depicted Marie-Antoinette in 1783. The fabric for the duchess's dress was apparently imported from England in flagrant violation of Spain's protectionist laws.[19] The dress bears a red sash, its color picked out in the bows that draw attention to her décolleté, her magnificently abundant coiffure, and the tail of her dog. This combination of red and white (the colors of the Basque festival of San Fermín) appears frequently in Balenciaga's work, perhaps nowhere more playfully than in his summer 1967 dress of Staron's stiff white Ziberline, its Empire bodice mischievously formed of two giant scarlet organza dahlias (pls. 42–43).

Balenciaga's Goya references can be overt, as in a winter 1948 cocktail dress of pink silk veiled in black lace (pl. 39), its attached collar recalling the fichu worn by the Duchess of Alba in her 1797 portrait, and in a summer 1962 evening dress with its frothy black lace bodice and gently high-waisted ivory skirt (pl. 36). A short, full-skirted evening dress of summer 1956 reveals the lower leg (pl. 35), as did the skirts of provocative Spanish ladies in the late eighteenth century. Christian August Fischer's *Travels in Spain in 1797 and 1798* documents the scandalously "short and fluttering petticoats, of which the long and transparent fringe exposes to view at every step a delicate and beautiful leg."[20]

Balenciaga's interpretations were sometimes oblique. For example, the puffy volume of his summer 1958 silk-gauze ball gown (pl. 40) suggests the costume worn by the Marquesa de Pontejos in Goya's portrait, its curious hybridization of French (the polonaise overskirt) and English (the

rustic straw hat) styles resulting in an ensemble that is unmistakably Spanish (pl. 41).

The mantilla, a traditional Spanish head covering, was a prized possession. According to an 1864 English document, "A Spanish woman's mantilla is held sacred by law, and cannot be seized for debt."[21] As the French visitor Alexandre Laborde noted in *A View of Spain* (1806), the mantilla could be held away from the wearer's face with a fan so that "it floats above her head, and flutters about her person; it gives prominence and brilliancy to her eyes."[22] Otherwise it was raised and supported by a pad "kept in its place by a comb or a riband." Narcisa Barañana de Goicoechea, in a portrait attributed to Goya (pl. 15), wears an elaborate cockade of blue and black ribbons from which her lace-edged silk mantilla falls. Isabel de Porcel's mantilla is held by black ribbon in Goya's portrait from before 1805 (pl. 37).

For a winter 1967 dress with a remarkable cape (pl. 47), Balenciaga appears to have reinterpreted the form of the black lace mantilla that the Duchess of Alba wore over her voluminously dressed hedgehog coiffure in the 1797 Goya portrait. This extraordinary ensemble exemplifies the increased abstraction of Balenciaga's work in the 1960s, a counterpoint to the client-friendly pieces that formed the principal part of a collection.

Gloria Emerson may have had Balenciaga's experimental fashions in mind when she wrote in the *New York Times* in 1967, "There is always a little moment of glee in every Balenciaga collection."[23] As Colin McDowell has observed, "Balenciaga's clothes were often light-hearted and humorous—in a deeply serious way."[24] He could be referring to the double puffball effect of the green gazar capelet and evening dress from winter 1961 that created a silhouette as unrelated to the body beneath it as the traditional Spanish farthingales (pls. 54–55).

"If Dior is the Watteau of dressmaking—full of nuances, chic, delicate and timely—then Balenciaga is fashion's Picasso," wrote Cecil Beaton in 1954. "For like that painter, underneath all of his experiments with the modern, Balenciaga has a deep respect for tradition and a pure classic line."[25] Richard Martin expanded on the comparison when he observed, "Like the artist Picasso . . . Balenciaga played with the abstraction of form and the revelation of the body as if these were two themes in a piece of music. . . . The result, too, was like Picasso's fascinating oscillation between abstraction and realistic representation, for Balenciaga offered a new form of fashion, not only an option for fashion to represent the figure faithfully but also to flatter the figure in a splendid semi-fitted succession of curves, construction, fabric and cut."[26] Both Picasso and Balenciaga were inspired to rework Velázquez's *Las meninas* in some way (see pl. 50). They also shared a passion for black pearls, which Picasso felt resembled his eyes.[27]

From the late 1950s Balenciaga's experiments with form and with dynamic prints were paralleled by his increasing engagement with the world of contemporary art, which became more profound through his friendship with the distinguished collectors Aimé and Marguerite Maeght.[28] His compelling four-point gazar cocktail dress of winter 1967 (pl. 59), for instance, shares its aerial profile with an element in Joan Miró's automatist *Painting (Blue)* of 1927 (pl. 58).

Balenciaga may not have considered himself an artist, but the high regard in which his artist contemporaries held him is evidenced in tributes such as *Homage to Balenciaga*, a monolithic 1990 iron sculpture by Chillida.[29] Miró, a near contemporary of Balenciaga, created a work incorporating the designer's name that was used for the cover of the catalogue (pl. 53) accompanying Balenciaga's posthumous 1974 exhibition at the Palacio de Bibliotecas y Museos in Madrid—a tribute from one great Spanish creative force to another.

Richard Avedon
Suzy Parker wearing evening dress of black lace, winter 1952
Originally published in *Harper's Bazaar*, October 1952

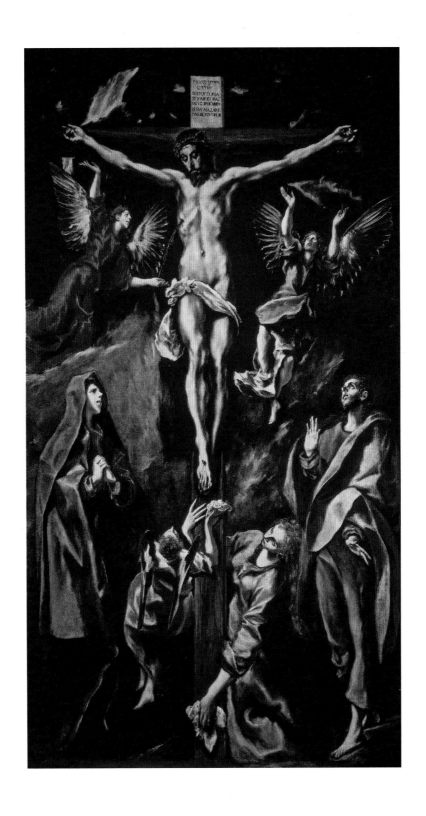

17
Domenikos Theotokopoulos (El Greco)
The Crucifixion, 1597–1600, oil on canvas
Museo Nacional del Prado, Madrid

18
House photograph of evening dress of black wool with taupe
silk-shantung draped bodice, hip swag, and train, summer 1950

Balenciaga
25 Avril 1950
167

19
Eric (Carl Erickson)
Evening dress of black wool with straw-yellow satin drape, winter 1951
Originally published in *Vogue*, December 1951

20
Francisco de Zurbarán
The Annunciation, 1638–1639, oil on canvas
Musée de Peinture et de Sculpture, Grenoble, France

21
House photograph of evening dress of gray silk satin, winter 1963

22
Clifford Coffin
Evening dress of gray velvet and taffeta, winter 1948
Originally published in *Vogue*, November 1, 1948

23
Francisco de Zurbarán
Saint Casilda, 1640, oil on canvas
Museo Nacional del Prado, Madrid

24
House photograph of evening dress of ivory silk with white beaded
embroidery by Bataille and pink taffeta bow, summer 1951

25–26
House photographs of evening dress of pink silk gazar, winter 1965

76

27
Evening dress of white organza with embroidered and appliquéd cotton roses by Lesage, summer 1958
Archives Balenciaga, Paris

28
Francisco de Zurbarán
Saint Francis of Assisi or *The Miracle of the Roses*, 1630, oil on canvas
Museo de Cádiz, Spain

29
Diego Velázquez
Infanta Margarita, 1653, oil on canvas
Musée du Louvre, Paris

30
George Hoyningen-Huene
"Infanta" evening dress of ivory silk satin and black silk velvet, winter 1939
Originally published in *Harper's Bazaar*, September 15, 1939

31
Richard Avedon
Doe Avedon wearing suit of white linen with black lace trim, summer 1948
Variant originally published in *Harper's Bazaar*, May 1948

32
Francisco de Goya
The Duchess de Alba, 1797, oil on canvas
The Hispanic Society of America, New York

33
Studio drawing of ball gown of black tulle, silk-satin ribbons, and silk fringe tassels, winter 1957

BALENCIAGA

(Photo Eugène Rubin.)

LA DENTELLE DE COTON *ornant une robe du soir est une des trouvailles de la collection de Balenciaga. On la voit ici sur une robe de piqué blanc : elle forme un plastron et un volant à la jupe. Cette robe photographiée ici de face et de dos est en outre garnie de rubans de velours rose disposés en bretelles et en nœuds. La ceinture est en ruban de velours rose. Bijoux de Boucheron.*

29

34
Eugène Rubin
Evening dress of white piqué and cotton lace with pink velvet straps and bows, 1938
Originally published in *Femina*, July 1938

35
House photograph of evening dress of ruched white tulle with black flowers, summer 1956

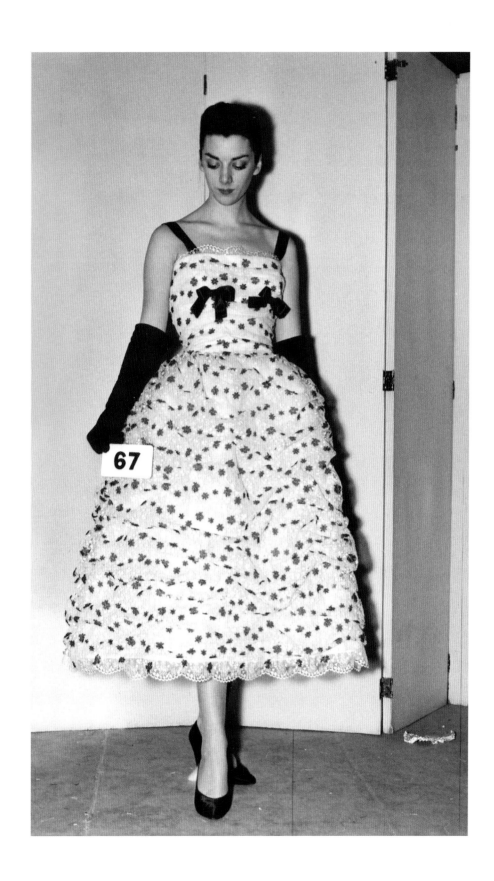

36
Cecil Beaton
Evening dress of ivory silk gazar and black lace, summer 1962

37
Francisco de Goya
Doña Isabel de Porcel, before 1805, oil on canvas
National Gallery, London

38
Francisco de Goya
Doña Tadea Arias, 1793–1794, oil on canvas
Museo Nacional del Prado, Madrid

39
Cocktail dress of rose peau de soie and black lace, winter 1948
Fine Arts Museums of San Francisco, gift of Mrs. C. H. Russell

40
House photograph of evening gown of turquoise silk gauze, summer 1958

41
Francisco de Goya
The Marquesa de Pontejos, ca. 1786, oil on canvas
National Gallery of Art, Washington, Andrew W. Mellon Collection

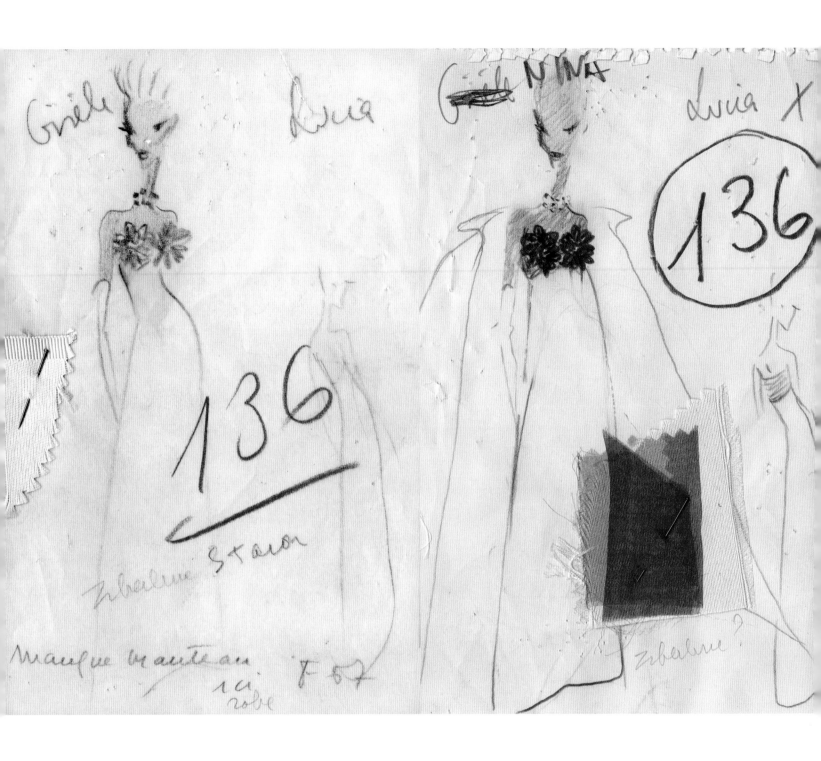

42–43
Studio sketches of evening dress of white Ziberline, red silk taffeta, and red silk organza, summer 1967

44
Francisco de Goya
The Duchess of Alba, 1795, oil on canvas
Collection of the Duchess of Alba, Madrid

45
House photograph of evening dress of black tulle and black and yellow lace, winter 1951

46
Spanish *maja* dress of light yellow, red, and yellow silk satin with overskirt of black pom-pom net, ca. 1801
Museo del Traje, Madrid

47
Irving Penn
Sue Murray wearing evening dress of black silk crepe with "chou" wrap of black silk gazar, winter 1967
Originally published in *Vogue*, September 15, 1967

48
Helmut Newton
Dress of navy-blue silk gazar and white organdy, summer 1968
Originally published in *Vogue*, March 15, 1968

49
Pablo Picasso
Seated Harlequin, 1901, oil on canvas
The Metropolitan Museum of Art, New York, purchase, Mr. and Mrs. John L. Loeb, 1960

50
Pablo Picasso
Las meninas, 1957, oil on canvas
Museu Picasso, Barcelona

51
House photograph of dress of black and white cloqué organza, winter 1951

52
David Bailey
Evening ensemble of black silk gazar, summer 1967
Originally published in *Vogue*, July 1, 1967

53
El mundo de Balenciaga, exhibition catalogue, 1974
Cover art by Joan Miró

54
Tom Kublin
Evening ensembles with dresses and capelets of forest- and lime-green silk gazar, winter 1961

55
House photograph of evening ensemble with dress and capelet of forest-green silk gazar, winter 1961

56
House photograph of evening dress of lime-green silk gazar, winter 1967

57
House photograph of evening coat of kelly-green silk faille, summer 1965

58
Joan Miró
Painting (Blue), 1927, oil on canvas
Musée National d'Art Moderne, Centre Georges Pompidou, Paris

59
Hiro
Cocktail dress of black silk gazar with rhinestones and faux pearls, winter 1967
Originally published in *Harper's Bazaar*, September 1967

60
Diego Velázquez
Philip III, King of Spain, ca. 1634–1635, oil on canvas
Museo Nacional del Prado, Madrid

ROYAL COURT

The dress of Spain's monarchs, their families, and their courtiers, depicted in some of the most striking portraiture in the history of art, exerted a powerful effect on Balenciaga's creative imagination. The regal costume of the five previous centuries informed his own designs for royalty and nobility—including the queen mother Maria Christina, Victoria Eugenia, and Fabiola de Mora y Aragón, the granddaughter of the Marquesa de Casa Torres, that most influential figure in Balenciaga's life—as well as his collections.

Two of Balenciaga's wedding dresses for brides marrying into royal families show allusions to the styles favored by Isabella I in the late fifteenth century. For the December 1960 wedding of Doña Fabiola to King Baudouin I of Belgium, Balenciaga created a full-skirted dress in heavy silk twill, trimmed at the neckline and along the seam at the low waistline with horizontal bands of white mink, which also edged the shoulder-hung cathedral train. This trimming recalls Queen Isabella's special fondness for ermine, a fur associated with royalty by medieval tradition. Her wardrobe accounts indicate that in 1495 timbers—600 skins—were dressed and worked into *tiras* (strips) to embellish the necklines and hemlines of her garments.[1] The 1515 bridal list of the queen's granddaughter, Isabella of Portugal, records a black velvet *saya* (court dress) trimmed with 240 ermine pelts—a combination of fabric and fur that Balenciaga evoked in the black velvet evening dress he created for Claudia Heard de Osborne around 1964, its bustled back lavished with ermine tails (pl. 82).[2] Moreover, the perpendicular style associated with Isabella's reign was recalled in Balenciaga's princess-line evening gowns of the 1960s and reached an apotheosis in his final design: the wedding dress that he created for María del Carmen Martínez-Bordiú y Franco's marriage to Alfonso de Borbón y Dampierre, the grandson of Alfonso XIII, in 1972 (pl. 14).[3]

Balenciaga's work seems to reverberate most powerfully with echoes of the regal dress of Spain's golden age, which dawned after the conquests of Mexico (1519) and Peru (1532), when the newly united country's military might seemed invincible and its wealth unmatchable.[4] When Philip II inherited the crown from his father, Charles V, who abdicated in 1556, "his empire embraced the whole face of the earth and he had subjects and vassals in all the four corners of the world."[5] Spain became "the arbiter of the world,"[6] and its royal fashions—the "Spanish etiquette"—dominated the courts of Europe for a century, supplanting the more sensuous costume of the Italian Renaissance.[7]

The profoundly pious character of Philip II set the pattern for the regal austerity so characteristic of Spanish dress, which is notable for its use of black, a color symbolic of renunciation. Charles V "saw black as a majestic color worthy of his rank and power, but also a virtuous color, a symbol of humility and temperance." For his son, black was the symbol "of all Christian virtues."[8] It was also, perversely perhaps, a signifier of wealth. Fallibilities in dyeing techniques meant that blacks of the medieval era were rarely true blacks but often closer to deep blue, brown, or gray. Cloth dyed employing these impoverished means was uneven in tone and its color fugitive, and thus its use was limited to clothing for the lower classes and for penitence and mourning, the latter a convention that would continue in Spain throughout Balenciaga's lifetime.[9] Gradually, more intense black dyes were developed, based on harvesting the oak gall, or oak apple.[10] However, their manufacture was a costly procedure,

and cloth dyed a deep, rich, and true black was thus the preserve of the ruling classes. Under Philip IV in the first half of the seventeenth century, the *vestido de color* (colored dress) was forbidden, and even foreigners were received only if dressed in the approved black costume.[11]

The particular character of Spanish dress was determined in no small part by the sumptuary laws enacted by various monarchs. These limited the use of certain fabrics, colors, furs, and embellishments to the court, as in the case of ruffs in the sixteenth century, which were reserved for ladies of royal birth.[12] A Balenciaga theater suit of winter 1945 recalls the sixteenth-century fad for bands of silk or velvet in a contrasting material to that of the garment.[13] In 1537 a disapproving Charles V attempted to limit the use of these decorations: "On *sayas* women may not wear bands more than four fingers wide, and not more than eight of them from top to bottom; or in place of each band, two or three strips (*ribetones*) requiring no more silk than one band. . . . Of silk *pestañas* ["eyelash" bands, so called because of their perforated edges] women may have as many as they wish on their *ropas* (coats). But this provision is not to be understood as extended to public women, who may not wear silk at all."[14] These laws continued through the centuries.

"For me, Balenciaga is El Escorial," said François Lesage.[15] The master embroiderer's metaphor hints at the duality in Balenciaga's work, combining as it does the splendor of Spain's historical court dress and the powerful ritual and mysticism of its Catholic Church. El Escorial, built by Philip II in the sixteenth century, after descriptions of the Temple of Solomon, was conceived at the height of Spain's imperial power. Dedicated to the third-century martyr Saint Lawrence, it was at once a monastery, a royal palace, and a mausoleum.[16] It also became a repository and showcase for the nation's art, housing numerous masterworks by El Greco, Juan Pantoja de la Cruz, and Diego Velázquez.

The majesty of late-sixteenth- and early-seventeenth-century Spanish court dress as illustrated in portraiture—particularly in the royal portraits by Pantoja de la Cruz (see pl. 72) and his successor Velázquez—was nowhere captured more vividly by Balenciaga than in the costumes he created for the actress Alice Cocéa for her role as Doña Fabia Oliveira in a 1941 production of *Échec à Don Juan* at the Théâtre des Ambassadeurs in Paris (see pl. 76). Amid the privations of occupied Paris, Cocéa "had wanted to mount the most dazzling spectacle, the most luxurious, the most magnificent," noted *Le Figaro*. "She insisted upon striking costumes, she demanded an orgy of colors, ordered a riot of fabrics . . . precisely at a time when fabrics are hard to come by, colors limited, toilettes are poor and décors are drab."[17] The embroidery that he lavished on Cocéa's costumes is similar to that produced for the designer by distinguished houses such as Lesage, Rébé, Bataille, and Métral. Balenciaga's superb costumes, which remained a source of pride to him throughout his life, suggest a close study of the appliquéd embroideries and voided velvets in black and other rich, dark colors that are emblematic of Spain's golden age.[18] In the sixteenth century, Spain competed with Italy for dominion in the production of sumptuous silk velvets.

Velázquez's 1652 portrait of Queen Mariana (pl. 75), the second wife of Philip IV, was the direct source for the ensemble that Balenciaga created for his client Madame Bemberg to wear to a costume ball given by

Étienne de Beaumont in 1939.[19] He substituted crimson for the queen's black velvet, possibly at the request of the client.

Balenciaga referenced painterly source material for his contemporary eveningwear as well. Balenciaga was even inspired by the farthingales, or hooped petticoats, that were a distinctive feature of Spanish court dress for three centuries. They appear to have been introduced by Juana of Portugal, queen of Castile, in the third quarter of the fifteenth century, seemingly to disguise an indiscretion. When the Portuguese princess Isabella received the Burgundian ambassadors in 1473, she wore a crimson velvet gown supported by green hoops.[20] The conservative Spanish court retained the farthingale until the early seventeenth century, when it was transformed into the extremely wide-skirted *guardainfante* depicted by Velázquez in his portraits of Queen Mariana and of the infantas Margarita (pl. 29) and María Teresa. Balenciaga used a kind of farthingale to support the skirts of his celebrated "Infanta" gown of winter 1939 (pl. 30) and exaggerated the idea further still for a 1943 evening dress. By 1950, he had abstracted and reduced the farthingale form to the six-point peplum of a strapless bodice, whose elaborate silk-cord embroidery by Ginisty and Quenolle is counterpointed by layers of airy silk tulle in the ball gown's skirts (pl. 78).

The shape of the *guardainfante* was mirrored in the elaborate coiffures, built out on frameworks and embellished with plumes and galloon bows, that were worn by royal ladies. Balenciaga allowed himself an antic moment in a summer 1966 hat in which airy ostrich fronds were fashioned to suggest these astonishing headdresses (pl. 74). To complement the Infanta gowns in his winter 1939 collection, he used headpieces formed of both curled ostrich plumes and clusters of sable tails. And for a summer 1962 evening dress (pl. 73), Balenciaga abstracted the source material further still—as was characteristic of this late period in his career. On a dress of thoroughly contemporary form, he scattered stiff, silvery tissue bows of the type that were used for these hairstyles and also for trim in the gowns of Mariana and Philip IV's infantas.

Balenciaga clearly looked to the costumes in portraits of Spain's kings and princes as well as those of its queens and infantas. Philip II's piety did not preclude an interest in personal adornment. He "dresses with such taste that one cannot imagine more perfection," wrote a Venetian observer in 1560.[21] When the king welcomed his third wife, the French princess Isabelle de Valois, to Guadalajara in January of that year, he was splendidly dressed in a white doublet trimmed with hammered gold, a short cape embroidered with gold and precious stones, and a black cap trimmed with white plumes.[22] Balenciaga used just such a cap, in crimson velvet with a black plume, to offset the rigorous tailoring of a black suit from winter 1950; Irving Penn photographed it on Régine d'Estribaud for his first cover of French *Vogue* (pl. 61). Drawing on a ca. 1558 portrait of Don Carlos (Philip II's eldest son), he interpreted the sitter's short cape lined in princely lynx for his own lynx-lined cape of winter 1950. These capes, another sixteenth-century fashion that was originally distinctively Spanish, are further evoked in Balenciaga's magnificent burgundy silk velvet coat from winter 1950 (pls. 62–63). Created from one shaped piece folded back on itself, the garment's double cape collar sets away from the wearer's nape, thus exaggerating the line of the neck in the manner Balenciaga favored. Its shape also echoes the falling band worn by the king in the 1644 portrait *Philip IV at Fraga* by Velázquez. This collar, which supplanted the small, stiffened, and upstanding ruff worn by the king a decade earlier, appeared again in Balenciaga's splendid ensemble of black watered silk and velvet from winter 1951 (pl. 77); its bodice beneath the jacket is formed of thick ivory cotton lace similar to that used to trim Philip IV's falling collars.

The later sobriety of Philip II's costumes was not extended to those of the royal ladies. In an enchanting small panel painting from the 1580s in the collection of the Hispanic Society of America, New York (pl. 65), the king, in black relieved only by the narrow frill of white in his ruff, sits before his daughters, the infantas Isabella Clara Eugenia and Catalina

Micaela, who are dressed magnificently in similar crimson robes embroidered with pearls.[23] Balenciaga reinterpreted this device in a winter 1954 evening dress of scarlet velvet scattered with artificial pearls of various sizes (pl. 64).

Balenciaga's winter 1949 cuirass bodice (pl. 69), with its impasto embroidery by Bataille, suggests the armor worn by Spain's monarchs and courtiers.[24] In the early 1960s Balenciaga began to make tunic-form garments that are given a distinctly armorial effect through the use of hammered and waffle-textured metallic lamé fabrics, created by houses such as Abraham and Nattier. Balenciaga's winter 1967 cocktail dress in yellow silk cloqué lamé (pl. 67) even has the illusion of buttoned-on sleeves, recalling the riveted arm articulations of the armor depicted in Antonis Mor's 1549 portrait of the Duke of Alba (pl. 66)—the "unbending diplomat and shrewd tactician" who became a favorite of Charles V.[25] The broad bow at the neck of Balenciaga's dress provides a softening contrast in the same way that the duke's scarlet silk sash plays off the martial strength of his armor.

In 1959 Balenciaga commissioned the sculptor Janine Janet to create three figures for display in the windows of the new boutique at 10, avenue George V. *The King* (pl. 70), *The Queen* (pl. 71), and *The Knave*, their armor suggested by bristling nail heads, reveal Janet's imagination and creative use of everyday materials.[26] The Lesage embroidery of a winter 1964 evening gown (pl. 68), thickly encrusted with paillettes and beads in tones of deep bronze and verdigris, also conveys a sense of the chased steel in sixteenth-century armor, its gleam traditionally dimmed by blackening.

By the late seventeenth century, Spain's power had waned through economically disastrous wars and inept Hapsburg rule, and the court's supremacy as arbiter of European style declined with it.[27] In its stead, the court of Louis XIV at Versailles, with its near-fetishistic obsession with the niceties of dress, style, and etiquette, became the de facto arbiter of regal and aristocratic taste in all things. The French influence was further disseminated in Spain with the advent of the Bourbon (Borbón) dynasty, which began in 1700 when Philip V, Louis XIV's grandson, assumed the throne of Spain. Philip, who was born in Versailles, was responsible for rebuilding Madrid's Royal Palace (which had been destroyed by fire in 1734) in high Baroque style, laying claim to the greatest royal residence in Europe. Under the Bourbon monarchs, Spain thus looked to France to set the styles.[28] Its national character, however, was too strong to have completely subsumed itself to French royal, and later imperial, fashions.

For instance, Francisco de Goya's early-nineteenth-century depictions of Queen María Luisa reflect, as costume historian Aileen Ribeiro has noted, "the distinctive Hispanicizing of French modes . . . that was manifested in a love of jewelry—the queen loved to show off her diamonds—and a fondness for the glitter of gold and silver lace."[29] María Luisa's granddaughter, Isabella II, shared this fondness, as her 1843 portrait by Vicente López y Portaña (pl. 80) reveals. In a 1960 evening gown by Balenciaga (pl. 79), the exquisite embroidery (attributed to Rébé) is rendered in golden paillettes whose luster is dimmed by the silk threads in which they are wrapped.[30] The gown's bell-shaped skirt echoes Isabella's; here, as always, the designer allowed the fabric of the skirt to fall unlined, revealing the material's natural properties. Balenciaga's magisterial evening gowns and wedding dresses, although they may have been created in France, remain essentially Spanish in character—dignified, hieratic, and regal.

61
Irving Penn
Régine d'Estribaud wearing suit of black wool, stole of green wool, and hat
of crimson velvet and black ostrich feathers, winter 1950
Variant originally published on the cover of French *Vogue*, October 1950

ensembles: *here, ruby*   *and sapphire*

Balenciaga used jewel brilliance, billowing line
reminiscent of the late Renaissance. Left, a sapphire velvet coat
with a deep shrug collar, gathered-in sleeves;
under it, a sapphire lace dress. Right, a great ruby
velvet coat with a double cape collar; under it, a ruby lace dress.
I. Magnin, California; Morgan of Montreal, Canada.

62
René Gruau
Evening coat of burgundy silk velvet, winter 1950
Originally published in *Flair*, October 1950

63
René Gruau
Evening coat of burgundy silk velvet, winter 1950
Originally published in *L'Officiel*, October 1950

Balenciaga aime les velours aux
tons précieux. Pour ce manteau du
soir à la double pèlerine, il a
choisi un beau velours cerise dont
le coloris est infiniment séduisant.
Les larges manches sont allurées.

64
Studio sketch of evening dress of red velvet and faux-pearl embroidery by Lisbeth, winter 1954

65
Artist Unknown
Philip II, King of Spain, and His Children, ca. 1583–1585, oil on wood
The Hispanic Society of America, New York

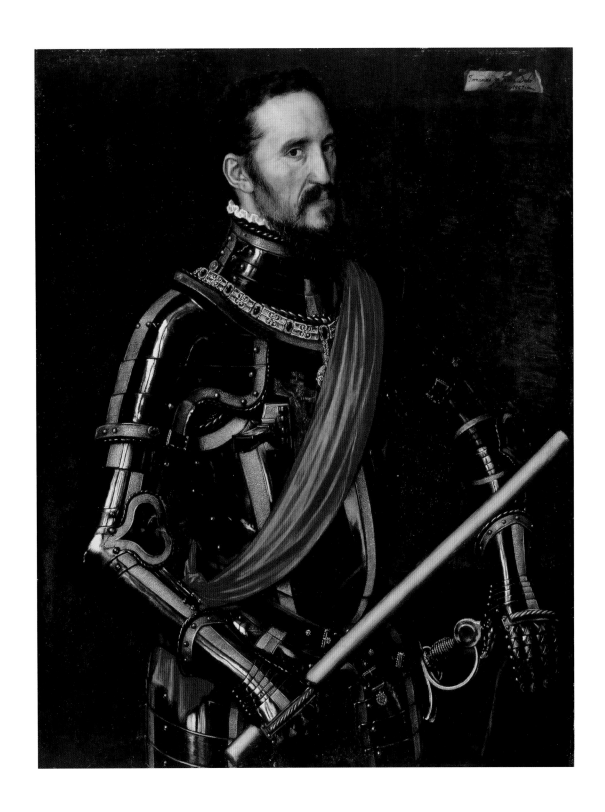

66
Antonis Mor
Fernando Álvarez de Toledo, Duke of Alba, 1549, oil on wood
The Hispanic Society of America, New York

67
House photograph of cocktail dress of yellow silk cloqué lamé, winter 1967

68
House photograph of evening gown with bronze and verdigris bead-
and-sequin embroidery by Lesage, winter 1964

69
Philippe Pottier
Evening dress of brown silk faille with beaded embroidery by Bataille, winter 1949
Originally published in *L'Officiel*, December 1949

70–71
Janine Janet
The King and *The Queen*, 1959, wood and nails
Les Arts Décoratifs, Musée de la Mode et du Textile, Paris

72
Juan Pantoja de la Cruz
Queen Isabelle de Valois, Third Wife of Philip II, 1605, oil on canvas
Museo Nacional del Prado, Madrid

73
House photograph of evening dress of gray cigaline with bead embellishment and bows, summer 1962

74
Tom Kublin
Hat of pink silk organza, ostrich feathers, and rhinestone brooch, summer 1966

75
Diego Velázquez
Queen Mariana of Spain, 1655–1660, oil on canvas
Kunsthistorisches Museum, Vienna

76
David Seidner
Theater costume of black silk velvet with sequin and bead embroidery by Ginisty and Quenolle, 1941
Archives Balenciaga, Paris, gift of Alice Cocéa

77
Henry Clarke
Cocktail ensemble of black moiré, ivory lace, and black velvet, winter 1951
Originally published in *Vogue*, September 15, 1951

78
Richard Avedon
Dovima wearing evening dress of champagne silk satin and pink tulle
with embroidery by Ginisty and Quenolle, winter 1950
Originally published in *Harper's Bazaar*, December 1950

79
Evening dress of embroidered gold silk satin with rhinestone embroidery by Rébé, 1960
Texas Fashion Collection, College of Visual Arts and Design,
University of North Texas, gift of Bert de Winter

80
Vicente López y Portaña
Queen Isabella II of Spain, 1843, oil on canvas
Museo Romantico, Madrid

81
Christian Franzen
Queen Victoria Eugenia, ca. 1910s

82
Evening gown of black silk velvet with bustle trimmed in ermine tails, ca. 1964
Texas Fashion Collection, College of Visual Arts and Design,
University of North Texas, gift of Claudia de Osborne

83
Francisco de Zurbarán
Saint Bonaventure Praying at the Election of the New Pope, 1628–1629, oil on canvas
Gemaeldegalerie Alte Meister, Staatliche Kunstsammlungen, Dresden, Germany

RELIGIOUS LIFE

The Church of San Salvador—built between the fourteenth and eighteenth centuries—rises in solemn Gothic majesty above the narrow streets at the medieval heart of Guetaria, its eight-sided bell tower clearly visible to returning fishermen and sailors. In the Spain of Balenciaga's childhood, religious authority went far beyond the church's commanding architectural presence. Catholicism had been the country's dominant religion since the Iberian Moors and Jews were forcibly converted or expelled by Isabella I and Ferdinand II in 1492.[1] With the Concordat of 1851, signed by Isabella II and the Vatican, Catholicism was enshrined in the country's constitution as "the only religion of the Spanish nation."[2] This agreement mandated, among other things, that education would conform to Catholic doctrine. Its tenets remained in place until the Second Spanish Republic was declared in 1931, although General Francisco Franco restored three of its articles with his own Vatican Concordat of 1953.[3]

The influence of the church was thus primal during Balenciaga's youth. His parents were deeply pious, and Balenciaga himself was a man of profound religious conviction and spirituality who contemplated following his uncle Julian Balenciaga, San Salvador's parish priest, into the clergy.[4] "For Balenciaga, designing clothes was more than a craft, more than art: it had the characteristics of a religious vocation," observed Eve Auchincloss, "and the power and purity of design that he achieved, working in isolation, inaccessible to press and public, seemed almost a form of prayer and sacrifice."[5] Balenciaga was seduced by the aesthetics of the Spanish mysticism of the sixteenth century, incarnated by influential Counter-Reformation figures such as Saint Teresa of Ávila founder of the Discalced (Barefoot) Carmelite sect, and her follower, Saint John of the Cross. In his farmhouse at Monte Igueldo, where he retreated after the intense work of each collection, Balenciaga created an interior "furnished with beautiful, rather uncomfortable, Spanish antiques" that self-consciously evoked the monastic world of these saints. According to Carmel Snow, it was an environment "as remote and simple as his personality."[6]

Balenciaga's habits were equally devout. In Paris, he went almost daily to celebrate mass at the church of Saint-Pierre de Chaillot, directly opposite his apartment on avenue Marceau, which coincidentally adjoined the Spanish embassy and was opposite the headquarters of the Basque Republic.[7] When he was thinking deeply, he would play unconsciously with a scrap of fabric in the same contemplative way that one caresses the beads of a rosary.[8] The salons and workrooms of his couture house were often compared to a house of worship, a monastery, or a convent. "His fashion house [had] a curious monastic seal," wrote José María de Areilza, "in which there was no room for loud and outspoken people, nor for laughter and disorder. Everything was done in an atmosphere of silence and efficiency."[9]

The ceremonial and everyday dress of the Catholic clergy—as well as its depiction in Spanish art—and the costumes of the church's sculptural devotional figures appear to have resonated deeply in Balenciaga's aesthetic consciousness. Above the side altars in the transepts of the Church of San Salvador are niches containing small eighteenth- and nineteenth-century figures of saints, made of carved and painted wood and elaborately clothed in brilliantly colored robes that are either carved or fashioned from textiles (see pl. 85). These sculptures mesmerized the young Balenciaga when he served as an altar boy, and echoes of the hieratic garments in which they are dressed reverberate in his creations throughout his career.[10]

As Judith Thurman has observed, Balenciaga "adapted the vestments of his parish church—the cope, the chasuble, and the *casulla*—for the wardrobe of the worldly woman."[11] From the beginning of his Paris career to his final collection for summer 1968, Balenciaga alluded to religious dress in elements of his work. For instance, his black silk ottoman evening coat from ca. 1939 (pls. 89–90), with its clerical collar and severe line, is a literal evocation of the contemporary priest's cassock, or soutane—the traditional form of quotidian wear established in the mid-nineteenth century (see pl. 91). The hand-stitched, mitered buttonholes and the triangular seams from waist to bust, which suavely accentuate the line, fail to mitigate the priestly rigor of a garment whose primary purpose was to provide an aesthetic foil (and modest cover) for the evening gown beneath it. This garment's silhouette was echoed that season in an evening coat of cardinal scarlet, retailed by Bergdorf Goodman, and another in white ottoman for a bridal gown.[12] Balenciaga's engagement with the cassock was enduring. For his summer 1952 collection he designed an example in heavy black silk twill (pl. 92); its hourglass form is exaggerated to conform to the mid-century ideal, but its attached capelet—suggesting a simar, or caped cassock—leaves little doubt as to its inspirational source. Balenciaga was evidently familiar not only with the look of a priest's cassock but also with its construction, as revealed by a letter he wrote to his sister Maria Augustina requesting the details of a soutane that he was making for the parish priest in Igueldo.[13]

A seventeenth-century nun's habit is suggested by the free-hanging back panel of a day dress from summer 1958 (pl. 99), shown in indigo linen but ordered by the client in chaste white. In his final collection, presented in 1968, Balenciaga added the flourish of a nun's linen veil (pl. 102) to a simple two-piece day dress of dark-blue linen. Balenciaga's remarkably austere wedding dresses from 1967 and 1968 (see pl. 100), which are brilliantly constructed from stiff silk gazar or zibeline, rely on minimal seams for their bold, sculptural presence. The headpieces with which they are worn repeat the lines of the nun's stiff veils and present an alternative to the traditional bridal veil. Even the pillbox hat—which transformed the millinery industry after Balenciaga introduced it in 1952—suggests the *zucchetto*, or skullcap, worn by clerics of the Catholic Church, as well as the black *boneta* or Spanish *biretta*. For a dress of deep-blue gazar from summer 1968 (pl. 101), Balenciaga interpreted the form of the chasuble as a shoulder cape and mirrored its shape in the full-length dress worn beneath it. He used the chasuble's traditional curved sides to reveal the ankle and lower calf, a decidedly immodest device that he had also experimented with in his embroidered black velvet dress from winter 1967 (pl. 93). Most of the clients who ordered this successful model (Claudia Heard de Osborne, Kitty Carlisle Hart, Mrs. Edward I. Hilson, and Mrs. Allan R. Johnson among them) wanted modifications to the height of the splits. "Balenciaga had a priest's *casulla* [chasuble] in mind when he cut this," noted Heard de Osborne of the dress. "He said, 'a very sexy priest.'"[14]

Balenciaga's brown gabardine raincoat from summer 1965 (pls. 86–87) is a relatively prosaic garment that the designer transformed into something extraordinary by giving it an overscale, pointed hood, recalling the brown hooded robes worn by Franciscan monks since the time of Saint Francis in the thirteenth century.[15] Balenciaga's likely source, Francisco de Zurbarán's various seventeenth-century depictions of Saint Francis (see pl. 28) show the saint wearing the homespun, ash-colored cruciform robe with a knotted rope belt (Balenciaga substituted tailored leather) and an attached pointed hood. This hood, which relates to that of the Moorish cape still worn in some rural areas of Morocco today, was later detached from the body of the robe, ultimately mutating into the *mozzetta*, or elbow-length shoulder cape, seen in Francisco de Goya's portrait of Cardinal Luis María de Borbón y Vallabriga (pl. 104). From the mid-fifteenth century Saint Francis was believed to have been "intact and standing" in his tomb, and it is in this astonishing attitude that Zurbarán depicted him in *Saint Francis Standing in Ecstasy* (ca. 1650-1856; Musée des Beaux-Arts, Lyon).[16] "It held the hands covered with the sleeves of the habit before its breast," as Pedro Ribadeneyra recorded in 1599; the resulting folds of his deep sleeves suggested Romanesque sculptures found in the Collegiate Church of Santillana del Mar.[17] This effect was repeated in Balenciaga's fawn cloth coat of winter 1950, depicted in Irving Penn's iconic study of his wife, Lisa Fonssagrives, for American *Vogue* (pl. 84). Balenciaga's color palette, too, was related both to the austere habits of monks and nuns and to the sumptuous vestments worn to celebrate the mass. Diana Vreeland was struck by Balenciaga's use of violet.[18] In church vestments violet symbolizes "the crucifixion and chastening of the body," while scarlet red "typifies fervor of spirit and charity, because the Holy Ghost descended upon the Apostles in fiery tongues—also blood shed for charity and faith."[19] Both colors recur often in Balenciaga's work.

To a magnificent black faille evening coat from winter 1954—its back fullness suggesting the depiction of religious vestments in seventeenth- and early-eighteenth-century Spanish painting—Balenciaga added deep pink buttons that recall a bishop's violet and black, red-trimmed cassock (pl. 95). Balenciaga repeated this coat's backward movement with his priestly cloqué evening coat from summer 1964, cut to the waist in front and forming a train in back (pl. 96). Bettina Ballard, while visiting Balenciaga in Igueldo, went to the thirteenth-century Gothic cathedral in nearby Burgos. "The wind sang in Burgos," she noted, "only the cathedral had a warmth—not a physical warmth, but a hot sort of grandeur from the very number of purple- and red-clad high clergy promenading under the stone protection of this most Catholic of Catholic cathedrals."[20] A double-tier coat of cardinal-red silk ottoman from winter 1954 (pl. 103) closely suggests the surplice depicted in Goya's painting of the cardinal (pl. 104). The allusion was subtly reinforced by the accompanying full-skirted dress with tiers of white lace, the ensemble's combination of color and texture echoing that of the cardinal's garments. Another literal evocation of these cardinal robes occurs in a winter 1965 ensemble of a cape worn over a sleeveless evening dress, this time in fuchsia (pl. 105).

Another potent reference point for Balenciaga was the magnificent robes created for the Madonna figures that are carried through the streets in Spanish cities and towns during the Holy Week festivities (see pl. 111). The importance accorded their raiment reflects the great reverence in which these figures are held. These robes, over which "a whole workshop of nuns or of laywomen has toiled several years," as Ruth Matilda Anderson wrote in 1957, could cost "thousands of dollars," at a time when a suit from the best tailor in Madrid, as Oscar de la Renta has related, cost eight dollars.[21] The tradition of dressing Madonna sculptures began in the sixteenth century. An example in the collection of the Metropolitan Museum of Art dates from the early seventeenth century.[22] The robe worn by this figure was adapted from the embroidered garment of an infanta. The coveted role of dresser and guardian of these figures was assigned to the *madrinas*, respected older women in the local community.[23]

Balenciaga was not only familiar with these figures (there is one in the Church of San Salvador), he also created the robes for one. His friend the art collector Marguerite Maeght asked him to dress the Madonna sculpture at Sainte-Roseline Chapel near Trans-en-Provence that she restored with the architect Josep Lluís Sert in 1959.[24]

The embellishment and sometimes even the silhouette of these robes find a parallel in some of Balenciaga's most magnificent creations. A beige taffeta dress of ca. 1946 (pl. 113), for instance, is embroidered by Lesage in metallic silver, gold, and steel-blue tinsel thread and seed pearls—materials often used in the robes of Madonna figures (seed pearls also occasionally describe the Virgin's tears). The concentration of embroidery at the bodice and hem and the repeating scattered motif on the rest of the dress also reflect the traditional treatment. The sumptuous embroidery by Métral of metallic leather and threads on a heavy ivory satin evening coat from winter 1953 evokes the magnificent woven textiles that were created in Mexico in the seventeenth century and exported to Spain, where they were used to dress Madonna figures and depicted in the lifelike religious figures sculpted by masters such as Juan Martínez Montañés and Francisco Ruiz Gijón.[25] Balenciaga showed this coat with a simple columnar evening dress of black wool, a characteristic play of opulence and austerity. A similar effect is achieved in a winter 1951 black wool evening dress with an attached stole of yellow satin (pl. 19) that provides a luxurious foil to the matte quality of the fabric and the simplicity of the dress's line. As Marie-Andrée Jouve has pointed out, this fall of golden silk closely resembles the treatment of the archangel's draperies in Zurbarán's *Annunciation* (1638-1639; pl. 20).[26]

A winter 1957 evening dress (pl. 112) is made in brocade woven to imitate watered, or moiré, silk, a fabric favored for liturgical vestments and used, for instance, in the *ferraiolo*, or floor-length cape, that indicates that its wearer is a member of the papal household or an apostolic nuncio.[27] Embroidered in ivory and gold, the dress features the innovative peacock-train silhouette that Balenciaga had just introduced, cut higher in the front and falling to floor-length (or even longer) in back. This gesture reflects the sweep of a Madonna's cloak that falls below the palanquin on which the figure is carried through the streets (see pl. 111).

"Folds of white chiffon or tulle encircle the sorrowing face and swathe the throat," noted Anderson of the Seville Madonna figure that Joaquín Sorolla y Bastida painted as a study for his painting at the Hispanic Society of America in New York, and there are a number of turn-of-the-century photographs of similar examples in the society's collections (see pl. 114).[28] Balenciaga captures this effect in his gold-embroidered black tulle hood from winter 1949 (pl. 116).

Liturgical textiles as well as robes provide inspiration. The scrolling carnation embroidery and eyelet cutwork of Balenciaga's oyster taffeta dress and bolero jacket of summer 1963 (pls. 107-108; a model originally presented with an enormous triangular stole instead of the bolero the client specified) relates closely to an eighteenth-century embroidered chasuble in the collection of the Fine Arts Museums of San Francisco (pl. 106).

But the most astonishing example of religious iconography in Balenciaga's work is perhaps his evening dress of winter 1959 in the collection of the Victoria and Albert Museum. Worn by the Best Dressed Hall of Famer Mrs. T. Charlton Henry of Philadelphia, the surprising dress is embroidered with an allover trellis motif of silver thread (pl. 110) that unmistakably suggests the crown of thorns, so powerfully emblematic of Christ's sufferings on the road to Calvary (see pl. 109). Although there is a trace of irony in a symbol of suffering being used on an evening dress destined for a life of luxury and pleasure, it was undoubtedly meaningful to Balenciaga, who worked with religious devotion to his craft.

Irving Penn
Lisa Fonssagrives wearing coat of fawn wool duvetyn, winter 1950
Originally published in *Vogue*, September 1, 1950

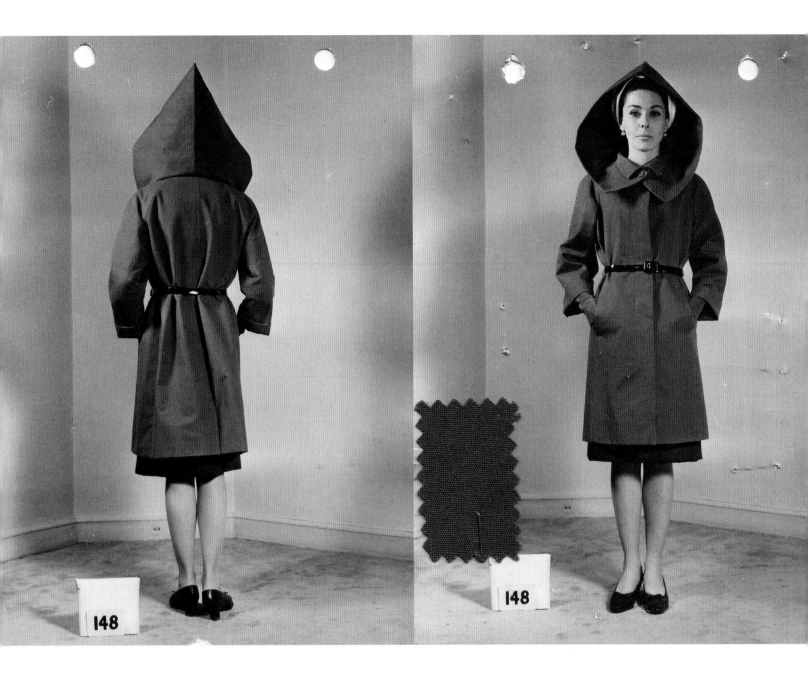

85 (preceding spread)
Church of San Salvador, Guetaria, Spain

86–87
House photographs of raincoat of brown gabardine, summer 1965

88
Domenikos Theotokopoulos (El Greco)
Saint Francis Venerating the Crucifix, ca. 1595, oil on canvas
Fine Arts Museums of San Francisco, gift of the Samuel H. Kress Foundation

89–90
Coat of black silk ottoman, ca. 1939
Collection of Hamish Bowles

91
Two priests in Barcelona, ca. 1900

92
House photograph of redingote of black silk twill, summer 1952

LES GRANDES LIGNES DE BALENCIAGA

Balenciaga une fois de plus cett[e]
saison a démontré qu'il était u[n]
grand maître de la Couture et qu[e]
tout ce qui était élégance étai[t]
son domaine incontesté. Les deu[x]
robes photographiées ici en fon[t]
foi de la façon la plus péremptoire[.]
Sur cette page, c'est un trè[s]
long fourreau de velours noir qu[i]
nous est proposé. Montant au ra[s]
du cou, il est orné sur les deu[x]
côtés d'une grosse broderie qu[i]
se répète au bas. Il est port[é]
avec des gants et des bas noir[s.]
Sur la page de droite, un modèl[e]
très différent du précédent. [Il]
est exécuté en crêpe blanc et [...]
une broderie d'argent qui bord[e]
les découpes de la taille. Jup[e]
longue soutenue par quelqu[es]
fines fronces. Décolleté ron[d]

93
Guégan
Evening dress of black velvet with rhinestone and bead embroidery by Rébé, winter 1967
Originally published in *L'Officiel*, October 1967

94
Francisco de Zurbarán
Holy Mass with Priest Cabañuelas, 1638, oil on canvas
Real Monasterio de Guadalupe, Cáceres, Spain

95
Studio sketch of evening coat of black silk faille, winter 1954

96
Studio drawing of evening ensemble with dress and jacket of black cloqué, summer 1964

97
Juan de Valdes Leal
Procession of Saint Clare, 1653, oil on canvas
Municipal Palace, Seville, Spain

98
Francisco de Zurbarán
Portrait of a Nun of the Jeronimite Order, 1638–1640, oil on canvas
Real Monasterio de Guadalupe, Cáceres, Spain

99
Studio drawing of day dress of indigo linen, summer 1958

100
House photograph of wedding dress and veil of white silk-satin organza and silk gazar, summer 1968

101
Neal Barr
From left: evening ensemble with bodice of black silk organza and
skirt of black silk gazar; evening dress of deep-blue silk gazar, summer 1968
Originally published in *Harper's Bazaar*, March 1968

102 (preceding spread)
Tom Kublin
Hat of white linen, summer 1968

103
Studio sketch of evening coat of scarlet silk ottoman, winter 1954

104
Francisco de Goya
Cardinal Luis María de Borbón y Vallabriga, after 1800, oil on canvas
Museo Nacional del Prado, Madrid

105
Evening ensemble with dress and cape of fuchsia silk faille, winter 1965
Los Angeles County Museum of Art, gift of the Estate of Mrs. John Jewett Garland

106
Spanish chasuble of linen, silk, and metal thread, 1725–1775
Fine Arts Museums of San Francisco, gift of Archer M. Huntington

107-108
Evening ensemble with dress and bolero of oyster silk taffeta
with embroidery and eyelet cutwork, summer 1963
Fine Arts Museums of San Francisco, bequest of Jeanne Magnin

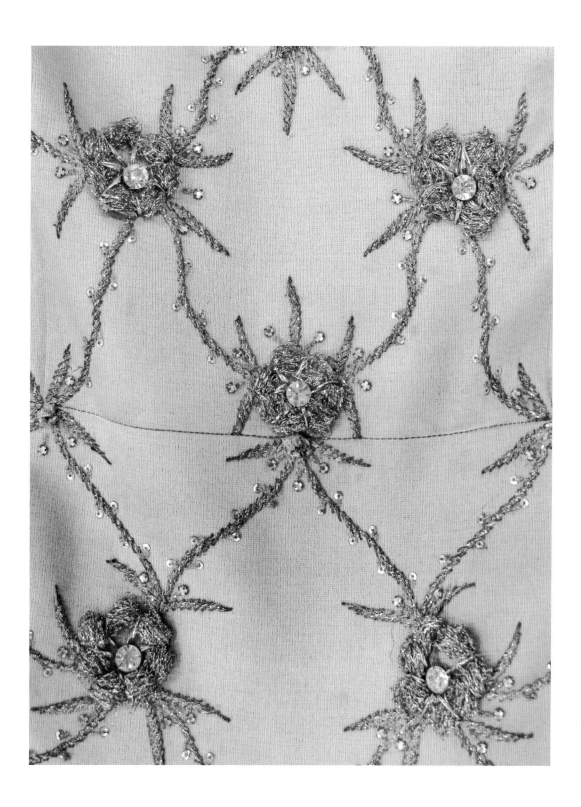

109
Domenikos Theotokopoulos (El Greco)
Christ Carrying the Cross, ca. 1580, oil on canvas
The Metropolitan Museum of Art, New York, Robert Lehman Collection, 1975

110
Evening dress of ivory silk satin with "crown of thorns" embroidery and rhinestones, winter 1959
Victoria and Albert Museum, gift of Mrs. Charlton Henry

N.º 334. Manto de Ntra Sra de la O. IGLESIA DE LA O.

111
Attributed to Emilio Beauchy
Mantle of Our Lady of O, ca. 1890

112
House photograph of evening gown of gold embroidered brocade
with underskirt of pale-blue taffeta, winter 1957

113
Evening dress of beige taffeta with metallic embroidery and pearls by Lesage, ca. 1946
Collection of Hamish Bowles

114
C. Sánchez del Pando
Our Lady of Refuge (Seville), ca. 1925

115
Artist Unknown
Virgin (*Imagen de vestir*), ca. 1825
Polychrome wood, costume and cape with gadroon and gilt-foil thread
embroidery and sequins, gilt-metal nimbus, and silver crown
The Hispanic Society of America, New York, gift of
Loretta H. Howard, in memory of her mother, Loretta Hines

116
Philippe Pottier
Headdress of black tulle with gold embroidery by Lesage, winter 1949
Originally published in *L'Officiel*, December 1949

117
Carmen Amaya performs interpretation of traditional Spanish gypsy dance, May 1, 1952

DANCE

Spain's extraordinarily rich dance culture and its history provided Balenciaga with a treasury of inspiration. Balenciaga would have known what has been called "the solemnity of Basque folk dance," with its intricate movements accompanied by the *irrintzi* (high-pitched cries) that bring to mind the celebratory or mournful ululations of North Africa and the Middle East.[1] The crowded Basque dance gatherings of the 1930s are depicted in the evocative paintings of José Arrúe Valle; the men's full-cut short jackets and blouses and the women's sprigged dirndl skirts and headscarves all find echoes in Balenciaga's work.[2]

Balenciaga would also have been familiar with the gaiety of Andalusian dance and possibly with the *quinta y pon* of Montehermoso, the energetic *jota fogueda* from Tarragona, and Spain's stylized religious narrative dances depicting the Passion of Christ, such as the *moixiganga*, which developed in the fifteenth century as a means of communicating with the preliterate populace.[3] However, it is to the Romantic tradition of the nineteenth century and to the drama of early- and mid-twentieth-century flamenco dance dress that Balenciaga returns again and again in his designs.

In the late eighteenth century, as the *majos* and *majas* were embracing Spanish regional dress, there developed a craze for the bolero dance. This dance, with its distinctive short jacket, was soon considered Spain's national dance. The country's dance tradition also became an important element of the Romantic ballet of the nineteenth century.[4] The great Italian dancer Maria Taglioni, the Austrian ballerina Fanny Elssler, the Danish Lucile Grahn, and the Italian Fanny Cerrito all performed *la cachucha*.[5] Balenciaga evoked the silhouette and embellishments of the costumes worn by these dancers in a brown velvet dress with elaborate black *madroño* (tassel) trim from winter 1943 (pl. 144).[6]

Marius Petipa developed Spanish themes for the Russian ballet with his choreography for *Don Quixote* (1869) and *Paquita* (1847, 1881); Pyotr Ilyich Tchaikovsky's *Swan Lake* (1877) and *The Nutcracker* (1892) each contain Spanish dance divertissements.[7] The Russian fascination with Spanish dance continued in the twentieth century. Sergey Diaghilev's Ballets Russes company was well received on a tour of Spain in 1916, and his experiences in the country encouraged him to work with Léonide Massine on the Spanish-themed ballet *Las meninas*, with music by Gabriel Fauré and designs by the great Spanish muralist José María Sert y Badiá.[8] Diaghilev had met the composer Manuel de Falla in Madrid, and their ensuing friendship led to their collaboration on *Le tricorne* (*The Three-Cornered Hat*). The ballet, which premiered in 1919, is based on Pedro Antonio de Alarcón's work, its music and choreography inspired by Andalusian folk-dance motifs. Massine included *farrucas*, *sevillanas*, fandangos, and a *jota* in the ballet. Joan Miró was keen to design this production, but Pablo Picasso was ultimately chosen.[9] Picasso's bold and dynamic designs, some produced during a stay in the Maria Cristina Hotel in San Sebastián, provide a compendium of Spanish costume styles, drawing on the regional dress of Aragón, Asturias, and Seville, as well as on traditional bullfight and flamenco dance costume.[10]

In Balenciaga's youth, the *cafés cantantes*, which had begun in the 1840s, were still popular entertainments. These cabarets brought flamenco dance traditions "from the caves and barrios to the stage."[11] The fierce beauty of flamenco performers and their dress had already captivated artists such as Gustave Doré, who in the 1860s produced a series of vivid studies of scenes in the Triana, Seville's Gypsy quarter, the center of Andalusian Gypsy music and flamenco dance.[12] Two decades later, John Singer Sargent captured the moon- and candlelit drama of flamenco in *Spanish Dancer* (study for *El Jaleo*) (ca. 1879–1882; pl. 124). Sargent depicted a dancer in the act of tossing back her head and sweeping back her skirt. The gesture of a dancer throwing her skirts to the side, the better to display some elaborate footwork, is vividly suggested by Balenciaga in his smoky-brown gauze dress of summer 1962 (pl. 125). The stiff body of the fabric enabled the designer to seemingly freeze the moment in time, as Sargent had done with bravura paint effects on canvas.

"The flamenco song is a wail of complaint from a people who has been repressed for centuries," wrote Ricardo Molina of the *soleá*, a fundamental type of flamenco music, in *Misterios del arte flamenco*. "Flamenco is the primal scream in its primitive form. . . . The tragedy of their song is not theater or an attempt to impress the audience. It is living tragedy."[13] The plaintive songs and the dance traditions of these marginalized people of Andalusian society resonated with cultural and intellectual figures in early-twentieth-century Spain, a time of social and political unrest.

The Gitanos (Spanish Gypsies) had been long persecuted. Even the *traje gitano* (Gypsy costume) had a dark history. Decrees issued by Philip II in 1560 and Charles II in 1695 prohibited Gitano women from wearing their traditional dress. The penalties for infringement included severe lashings and banishment.[14] In the eighteenth century even the word *Gitano* was banned by law.[15] In the 1920s the poet Federico García Lorca was at the vanguard of a movement of Spanish cultural figures, including De Falla and the artist Ignacio Zuloaga (see. pl. 133), who embraced the inherent poignancy of flamenco and encouraged its revival.[16]

In 1922 De Falla arranged a singing and dancing contest at the Alhambra in Granada to discover and promote local flamenco talent. The event inspired García Lorca to begin his *Romancero Gitano* (translated into English as *Gypsy Ballads*) and *Poema del cante jondo*. The contest captured the popular imagination to the extent that local movie theaters began to hold their own flamenco competitions after screenings.[17]

Meanwhile, La Argentina, born Antonia Merce in Buenos Aires to Spanish parents, "rejuvenated the dance in Spain," as flamenco expert Barbara Thiel-Cramér has noted, "at a time when the art of flamenco was being downgraded and the classical bolero dance was dying out."[18] Dressed by the costume designer Nestor, La Argentina brought flamenco dance forms to a wide audience, inspiring composers such as Isaac Albéniz, Enrique Granados, and De Falla to write music for her.[19] On her extensive world tours she captured the artistic imagination in much the same way that Loïe Fuller and Isadora Duncan had done before her. She also revived the art of the castanets, which Christian Bérard included in his sketch for *Vogue* of Balenciaga's winter 1946 toreador bolero (pl. 136).[20] Her influence, and those of her fellow dancers, was potent. In the Paris couture, designers including Jeanne Lanvin, Paul Poiret, and the house of Paquin's Ana de Pombo, a friend of Balenciaga's and a fellow Spaniard, drew inspiration from the flamenco dancer's *bata de cola* (dress with ruffled train). In the late 1930s De Pombo was especially celebrated for her overtly flamenco-inspired dresses, with their tiers of ruffles and dramatic trains.[21]

Under the Second Republic, many Spanish aristocrats left the country, and without their patronage, the cafés that employed flamenco performers began to close down.[22] Successful dancers such as Carmen Amaya (pl. 117), "an international cultural icon who combined fury with tenderness," took their talents on the road.[23] The civil war had a similar effect. Amaya embarked on a world tour, accompanied by the guitarist Sabicas, bringing her art to wider audiences in Latin America, Cuba, and North America.[24] She had danced before the king of Spain, defying protocol by looking him directly in the eye, and later performed for Queen Elizabeth II, Winston Churchill, and Franklin D. Roosevelt. She also appeared in films that further helped to draw attention to flamenco.[25] Amaya often wore the *traje corto*, the characteristic costume of the male flamenco dancer, to accentuate her aggressive, masculine dance style. She was known to put her shoes through the wooden stages on which she danced, so powerful were her flamenco taps.[26] Balenciaga often referenced the lines of the *traje corto*, with its close-fitting, cropped bolero jacket, cummerbund, and tight pants. A black crepe cocktail dress and cropped jacket from the late 1930s imitates this silhouette with a wide satin waistband that suggests a cummerbund.

General Francisco Franco later embraced Andalusian dance and song forms as a seductive and apolitical means of reinforcing a Spanish identity on the world stage.[27] Flamenco—whether performed by genuine Gitanos, classical ballet dancers, or dramatic entertainers—thus remained a vital part of Spanish culture. Balenciaga returned often to the idea of flamenco dance dress, refining and abstracting its characteristic elements. He even made a performance costume for the splendid Lola Flores, "more a popular singer than a strictly flamenco one," as Bernard Leblon has noted.[28] Although not born a Gitana, Flores considered herself *Gitana de adentro* (Gypsy in the heart and the gut). Balenciaga created for her a classic flamenco costume, with a vast *bata de cola* of stiffened ruffles, in a bold design of black *lunares* (large polka dots) on white.

The *bata de cola* dress was developed to extend the line of the flamenco dancer and exaggerate the rapid flip of her flounced train.[29] The celebrated dancer La Mejorana seems to have been the first dancer to wear it; she bequeathed her stage wardrobe to her daughter, the equally famous Pastora Imperio.[30] By the 1920s the *bata de cola* was an integral element of flamenco stage dress. "When handled with the expertise of a fine artist, it becomes an instrument for conveying a multitude of moods and nuances," wrote dance scholar Matteo Marcellus Vittucci.[31] Amaya used it for her celebrated gesture, the *coletazo en vuelta*, a lashing of the tail while turning.[32] The *bata de cola* was originally worn gathered up with ribbons into a bustle, and it appears to derive from the elaborately trimmed and trained skirts that were fashionable in the late 1870s.[33]

Balenciaga repeatedly evoked the flamenco dancer's skirt and its "long, graceful silhouette characteristic of a Cretan snake goddess."[34] He mimicked the precise effect of the *bata de cola* in a curvaceous black velvet evening gown from winter 1951 (pl. 130). Its skirts, sweeping to a train in back, are cut high in front to reveal the flamboyant tiered flounces of hot-pink silk that are sewn into its lining. By 1957, in a dress of black velvet with a molded torso (pl. 132), Balenciaga had reduced the idea of the flamenco ruffle to the single deep flounce that forms the skirt and an underlayer of black silk faille. He returned to this silhouette in summer 1966 for a gazar dress (pl. 131), this time with its skirt hem frothing with black organza petals.

Just as the line of the flamenco dance dress evolved with changing fashion—low-waisted in the 1920s, it became more sinuous in the 1930s and took on an hourglass shape in the late 1940s and 1950s—so, too, did Balenciaga's own increasingly subtle takes on the style. In his winter 1957 dress of hot pink taffeta, sketched for *Vogue* by René Bouché

(pl. 123), the skirt assumes pneumatic proportions, but its elaborately ruffled hem still betrays its origins.[35]

The dancers in Joaquín Sorolla y Bastida's wondrously atmospheric painting *Vision of Spain, Sevilla, the Dance* (1914; pl. 119) are not performing flamenco but instead the traditional dances that celebrated the weeklong festival of the Cruz de Mayo (Cross of May) following Holy Week.[36] During this week dancers traveled from house to house, accepting hospitality from the hosts and dancing in courtyards where elaborately decorated altars had been erected.[37] "Sevillians have a special genius for developing rituals," as Ruth Matilda Anderson observed, "in which the religious and the secular are fused, life to them being whole and indivisible."[38] Anderson posited that due to the presence of men at these festive ceremonies, "there developed a most feminine type of *sevillana*, fascinating in her grace of movement."[39] Anderson also remarked on "the frilly dress of percale or batiste, crackling with starch," worn by the dancers and guests in Sorolla's painting; Balenciaga achieved just this effect by using fabrics with a stiff, natural body of their own.[40]

Sorolla's dancers wear dresses patterned with delicate dots, distinguishing them from the Gypsies and stage performers who wore the bolder *lunares*, the giant polka dots that Balenciaga delighted in using. For instance, he used Ducharne's black-on-red polka-dotted chiné taffeta for a cocktail dress from summer 1962 (pl. 129). The fabric is wrapped around the body to end in a vertical double ruffle down the front; the accompanying cocoon cape is also edged in these double ruffles. Balenciaga's use of *lunares* reached its apotheosis in a satin organza dress of summer 1964 (pl. 127). Some of the polka dots were artfully cut out and reapplied over the center front seam to disguise its presence. In this dress, the *bata de cola* was abstracted into the flounce at the hem of a flying panel in back, which, in one of Balenciaga's beloved transformational gestures, can be lifted up to become a short cape.

The accessories of flamenco dress also inspired Balenciaga. Sargent's dancer flourishes a dark *mantón de Manila*; the dancers in Sorolla's painting wear pale examples of these silk shawls, embroidered with brilliantly colored floral designs. Spanish colonization of the Philippines began in 1565, and in Balenciaga's childhood much of the wealth of the Basque coast was still derived from trade with that country.[41] The lavishly embroidered *mantóns de Manila* were made in China but imported through the Philippines to Spain, where the fringing was added.[42] Their characteristic foliate embroidered designs began to appear in European fashion and decorative textiles from the early eighteenth century.[43] They eventually became an essential feature of flamenco dance dress, and of Sevillana costume, crossing the otherwise clearly defined class divide. The dancer Blanca del Rey was celebrated for her *soleá* with a vast *mantón de Manila*. "She dances with it as if it were a partner," noted Thiel-Cramér. "It swings around her, it embraces her, it spreads out in big patterns and it clings to her, a magnificent, extraordinary experience of beauty."[44]

In 1960 Balenciaga commissioned the embroiderer Lesage to re-create the distinctive silk floss embroidery of these shawls for a classical princess-line dress in stiff silk (pl. 120). Four years later he used a variant embroidery from the same house for an even more intriguing design, which suggests the bias effect that is achieved when the shawl is folded diagonally and the wearer takes advantage of its resulting elasticity to drape it close to her body. Other flamenco accessories were echoed in Balenciaga's witty and enchanting hats. These might take the form of a flower tucked into a dancer's knot of hair (pl. 134) or of a "knotted scarf hat," such as one striking example fashioned from a scarf in black *lunares* over hot pink and another of black tulle that simulates the dancer's hairstyle, its "chignon" tied with ribbon and tucked with rosebuds.

Henry Clarke
Evening dress of black silk taffeta and black lace, winter 1951
Originally published in *Vogue*, September 1, 1951

119
Joaquín Sorolla y Bastida
Vision of Spain, Sevilla, the Dance, 1914, oil on canvas
The Hispanic Society of America, New York

120
House photograph of evening dress of ivory silk with
polychrome silk floral embroidery by Lesage, summer 1960

121
José Ortiz-Echagüe
At the Seville Fair, 1950s

122
Studio drawing of evening dress of black silk gazar and silk flowers, summer 1961

123
René Bouché
Evening dress of pink silk taffeta, winter 1957
Originally published in *Vogue*, October 15, 1957

124
John Singer Sargent
The Spanish Dancer (study for *El Jaleo*), ca. 1879–1882, oil on canvas
Private collection

125
Studio drawing of evening dress of brown silk gauze, summer 1962

Seckers

126
José Ortiz-Echagüe
Andaluza, ca. 1950

127
Tom Kublin
Evening dress of white silk satin organza with black dots, summer 1964

128
Olé! Lola Flores
Record cover, ca. 1955

129
Tom Kublin
House photograph of cocktail ensemble with dress and cape
of red silk taffeta with black dots, summer 1962

130
Gjon Mili
From left: evening dress of black velvet and pink silk taffeta;
evening dress of black velvet and white tulle;
evening dress of black wool crepe with fuchsia satin drape, winter 1951

131
Studio drawing of evening dress of black silk gazar and silk organza, summer 1966

132
House photograph of evening dress of black silk velvet and black silk faille, winter 1957

133
Ignacio Zuloaga
Playing Guitar on the Balcony, ca. 1903, oil on canvas
Private collection

134
Cocktail hat of black silk taffeta with crimson silk rose, ca. 1955
Collection of Hamish Bowles

135
Joaquín Sorolla y Bastida
Vision of Spain, Sevilla, the Bullfighters, 1915, oil on canvas
The Hispanic Society of America, New York

160

THE BULLFIGHT

Balenciaga "hated bullfights," wrote Bettina Ballard, who noted that he only accompanied her to them out of politeness.[1] The form, colors, and embellishment of the bullfighters' traditional costumes, however, proved an enduring inspiration to the designer.

The *traje de luces*, that coruscating suit of lights that so ignites the bullring, was derived from liveries worn by servants who attended the aristocratic *rejoneadores*—mounted matadors—of the seventeenth century.[2] The legendary matador Joaquín Rodriguez, known as Costillares, who made his debut in Madrid in 1767 and is considered the originator of spectator bullfighting, is credited with formalizing its design.[3] An example of Costillares's signature ensemble of green silk, faced and trimmed with pink, if we are to believe the artist who hand-colored the plate, appears in *Colección de trajes de España* (1777–1788; pl. 149). In it he wears the snood and shortened jacket of the *majo*. The contrasting fabric at the top of his jacket's sleeves suggests the Renaissance fashion of revealing the undershirt between the ties attaching sleeves to the body of a garment. The sleeves of a bullfighter's jacket are fastened only at the shoulders to facilitate movement.[4] By the second quarter of the nineteenth century, as a portrait of Francisco Montes in *Tauromaquia completa* (1836) reveals, this feature had evolved into a pair of stiffened and elaborately embellished epaulettes.[5] The snood had been replaced by a *montera* hat and the neckerchief by a narrow *corbatín* tie; the wide sash (typical of Seville dress) and waistcoat were combined into a short vest of a single color; and the coat had mutated into the cropped bolero jacket, or *chaquetilla*, characteristic of the matador.[6]

By the mid-nineteenth century the *taleguilla* (knee breeches), cut tight enough to avoid a fold in the fabric that a bull's horn might catch, were also of a uniform color with the jacket and vest.[7] These breeches required dexterity on the part of a bullfighter's dressers, who had to lift them up for him. The ethnographer Ruth Matilda Anderson observed that the dressers sometimes had to stand on chairs on either side of the fighter for the final moments of the breeches' fitting.[8] The solemnity of the matador's dressing ritual—which could take more than two hours—parallels the painstaking toilette of the mid-century couture client.

Balenciaga grew up with bullfighting imagery all around him. According to the costume historian Miren Arzalluz, in 1883 San Sebastián became the first Spanish city to use posters to advertise bullfights.[9] Balenciaga must have been familiar with these seductive invitations to the bullring, with their promise of dashing performers and coquettishly dressed ladies in festive mantillas, their multicolored *mantóns de Manila* draped over the balconies of their boxes. "These images were soon to become part of the public imagination," remarks Arzalluz, "and, very possibly, part of Balenciaga's own store of ideas."[10] From his earliest collections, Balenciaga included designs that contain overt allusions to the costume of the matador. From his winter 1939 collection, *Harper's Bazaar* singled out "Goya's bullfighter snoods of crochet-work,"[11] such as the one depicted in a late-eighteenth-century Francisco de Goya portrait of the matador Pedro Romero dressed in an outfit presumed to have been given to him by the Duchess of Alba. In 1948 the same magazine rhapsodized about "the Spain of brilliant colors, beads, paillettes, pom-poms, and the little jacket of the matador" in Balenciaga's work.[12]

His designs also demonstrate an engagement with historical styles. For a deep blood-red velvet bolero jacket from winter 1946 (pl. 137), for instance, Balenciaga collaborated with the embroidery house Bataille to create elaborate spangled jet and silk-cord passementerie elements in imitation of the *alamar* (frog and braid trimming) created by the bullfighters' tailors, the *sastres de toreros*, in the nineteenth century. This bolero is closely related in color and decorative treatment to a matador costume of ca. 1885–1925 in the collection of the Museo del Traje, Madrid. The jacket's distinctive edging of *borlones*, or pom-pom tassels, was a device that Balenciaga used throughout his career—he had even incorporated them into the dress he made in 1912 for his cousin Salvadora Egaña Balenciaga's wedding.[13]

The winter 1946 bolero is a key element of the evening ensemble depicted in Christian Bérard's impressionistic watercolor for *Vogue* (pl. 136). Conflating the garb of a bullfighter with the stance of an Andalusian dancer, Bérard's subject brandishes her castanets to the accompaniment of a guitarist. In the nineteenth century this connection was forged by bullfighter-dancers such as José Ulloa, known as Tragabuches, a Gitano who boldly claimed "to kill two bulls and dance three dances" in an afternoon.[14] The twentieth-century dancer Vicente Escudero claimed that a performer could learn from the matador's highly stylized movements—perhaps referring to the balletic gestures known as the *veronica* and the *afarolado*, in which the arms are raised high in the graceful curving shape of a swan's neck.[15] "You bullfight and dance with the waist," the critic Gregorio Corrachano has written.[16]

In winter 1947 Balenciaga presented a matador bolero in pale-blue cotton velvet; the client Jean Sinclair Tailer ordered a version in ruby red that is now in the collection of the Costume Institute of the Metropolitan Museum of Art, New York (pl. 139). The broad shoulders of the 1946 design, accentuated by heavily decorated epaulettes that closely mimic those on matador jackets, had by then softened into the rounded, sloping line ordained by Christian Dior in his spring 1947 Ligne Corolle, or "New Look," collection. Yet the embroidery of the 1947 bolero, with its free-swinging tassel elements, is closer to that of the traditional *traje de luces*, such as the one worn by Juan Belmonte in Ignacio Zuloaga's moodily evocative 1924 portrait (pl. 140).[17] Balenciaga's winter 1943 velvet evening bodice and skirt (pl. 144), in his beloved combination of brown and black and featuring elaborate black *borlones*, seems to reference an early-nineteenth-century Andalusian *majo* jacket, of a type associated with equestrians and bandits, that was in Balenciaga's personal collection of historic costumes (see pl. 143).[18]

In the 1950s and 1960s Balenciaga continued to draw inspiration from bullfighting costume, but in this area, as in others, his allusions became more oblique. The *chaquetilla* might be reduced to an unembellished bolero jacket (pl. 152), or the brilliant yellow of the matador's cape evoked in an evening wrap constructed from a single square of fabric (pl. 153). *Borlones* are used not only to decorate but also to weigh the sleeves of a stately evening gown (pl. 145), are attached to the brim of a pillbox hat (pl. 146), or are scattered in seemingly random formation over a cape (pl. 150). The latter is surely a nod to the bullfighter's *capote de paseo*, or ceremonial cape, as shown in Zuloaga's portrait of Belmonte, its form derived from the traditional cape of Jerez.[19]

Balenciaga's clients were generally discouraged from adapting his designs, but the supremely elegant Pauline de Rothschild nevertheless made her own bravura intervention on a winter 1960 ensemble that Balenciaga presented as a ball gown in the characteristic bright pink of a matador's *medias* (stockings), worn with a matching bolero jacket weighted with oversize silk *borlones* at the hem (pl. 147). Rothschild amplified the matador allusion by wearing the jacket with a far more adventurous black satin romper suit that suggests the matador's knee breeches. This version of the ensemble accented Rothschild's legs, of which she was justly proud.

Balenciaga and his milliners, Vladzio Zawrorowski d'Attainville and Ramón Esparza, endlessly referenced matador headgear, often exaggerating and diminishing scale to playful effect.[20] These hats were often presented with clothes that otherwise bore little relationship to the costume of the bullring; sometimes they seem intended to enliven especially austere ensembles. The bullfighter's crocheted snood, which first appeared in the eighteenth century, is evoked in Balenciaga's ca. 1948 hat of black and white straw (pl. 141); it has been artfully embroidered to suggest pom-poms and the mesh that contains the *moña* (bun) into which a bullfighter's hair is dressed. In the second quarter of the nineteenth century, the snood—and the ribbons that attached it—was replaced by the *montera*. Joaquín Sorolla y Bastida depicted this hat form, with its bulbous side elements evoking a bull's horns, in his painting *Vision of Spain, Sevilla, the Bullfighters* (1915; pl. 135), and it remains the standard today. The *montera* is painstakingly composed of knotted black silk, frayed in imitation of hair. A hat could take forty days to make, fashioned entirely by hand.[21] Balenciaga shrank the *montera* into tiny pillboxes of straw and satin for his summer 1961 collections; in summer 1964 he exaggerated its scale to create a hat composed of large white tulle pom-poms. A hat from winter 1954 calls to mind the tiny plaited pigtail, or *añadido* (see pl. 159), that a matador wears until, upon his retirement from the ring, it is ceremonially cut off in a ritual known as *cortarse la coleta*.[22] Originally the bullfighter's own hair, this pigtail later became a separate element, a *castañeta*, that is attached to a flat, fabric-covered disc and is in turn affixed beneath the *montera*. Balenciaga replicated the disc and mimicked the plait, tied with a panache of yellow satin ribbons, with curled black ostrich feathers imitating the tip of the pigtail.

Nor did Balenciaga overlook the carnation, the flower traditionally thrown as a tribute to a matador considered to have performed well in the ring. It is a motif that appears again and again in his work. In a formal evening dress from winter 1957 (pl. 156), the subtlety of the carnations woven into the black silk damask is counterpointed by the bright-pink silk carnation that Balenciaga placed to accent the high waist. On a summer 1956 puffball evening gown (pl. 157), the warp-printed carnations seem, on their pale ground, like the flowers scattered on the clear yellow sand of a bullring in the blazing heat. Lest we forget, the carnation is the national flower of Spain.

136
Christian Bérard
Evening bolero jacket of blood-red silk velvet with jet and passementerie embroidery, winter 1946
Originally published in *Vogue*, November 15, 1946

137
Evening bolero jacket of blood-red silk velvet with jet and passementerie embroidery by Bataille, winter 1946
Collection of Hamish Bowles

138
Matadors Antonio Ordoñez and Luis Miguel Dominguín, Malaga, Spain, August 14, 1959

139
House photograph of evening bolero jacket of powder-blue cotton velvet
with black beaded embroidery by Rébé, winter 1947

140
Ignacio Zuloaga
Juan Belmonte, 1924, oil on canvas
Colección Zuloaga, Zumaia, Guipúzcoa, Spain

141
Hat of black and white straw, ca. 1948
The Museum at the Fashion Institute of Technology, New York, gift of Doris Duke

142
José Ortiz-Echagüe
Bullfighters, early 20th century

143
Spanish bolero of embroidered brown velvet, 19th century
Galliera, Musée de la Mode de la Ville de Paris, gift of Cristóbal Balenciaga

144
Evening ensemble of brown velvet with black embroidery and ball fringe, winter 1943
Galliera, Musée de la Mode de la Ville de Paris

145
House photograph of evening dress of black silk cloqué
with silk and jet bead-ball fringe, winter 1961

146
Cocktail hat of black silk satin with silk tassels and beads, ca. 1960
Collection of Hamish Bowles

147
House photograph of evening ensemble with dress and bolero
of pink silk faille with pink silk *pampilles* and beads, winter 1960

148
House photograph of evening jacket of black chenille with aqua sequins, winter 1964

149
"Joaquín Costillares," plate 28 in Juan de la Cruz Cano y Olmedilla, *Colección de trajes de España*, 1777–1788
The Hispanic Society of America, New York

D. Juan de la Cruz sculp.

Joaquin Costillares.   Le Fameux Joaquin Costillares.

150
Evening cape of black satin with pink *pampilles*, winter 1962

151
Henri Cartier-Bresson
Luis Miguel Dominguín in the bullring in Pamplona during the festival of San Fermín, July 1952
Originally published in *Harper's Bazaar*, May 1953

152
Evening ensemble with dress of black Ziberline and bolero of pink silk gazar, summer 1966
Fine Arts Museums of San Francisco, the Eleanor Christensen de Guigne Collection
(Mrs. Christian de Guigne III), gift of Ronna and Eric Hoffman

153
House photograph of evening wrap of yellow silk with black silk satin bows, summer 1965

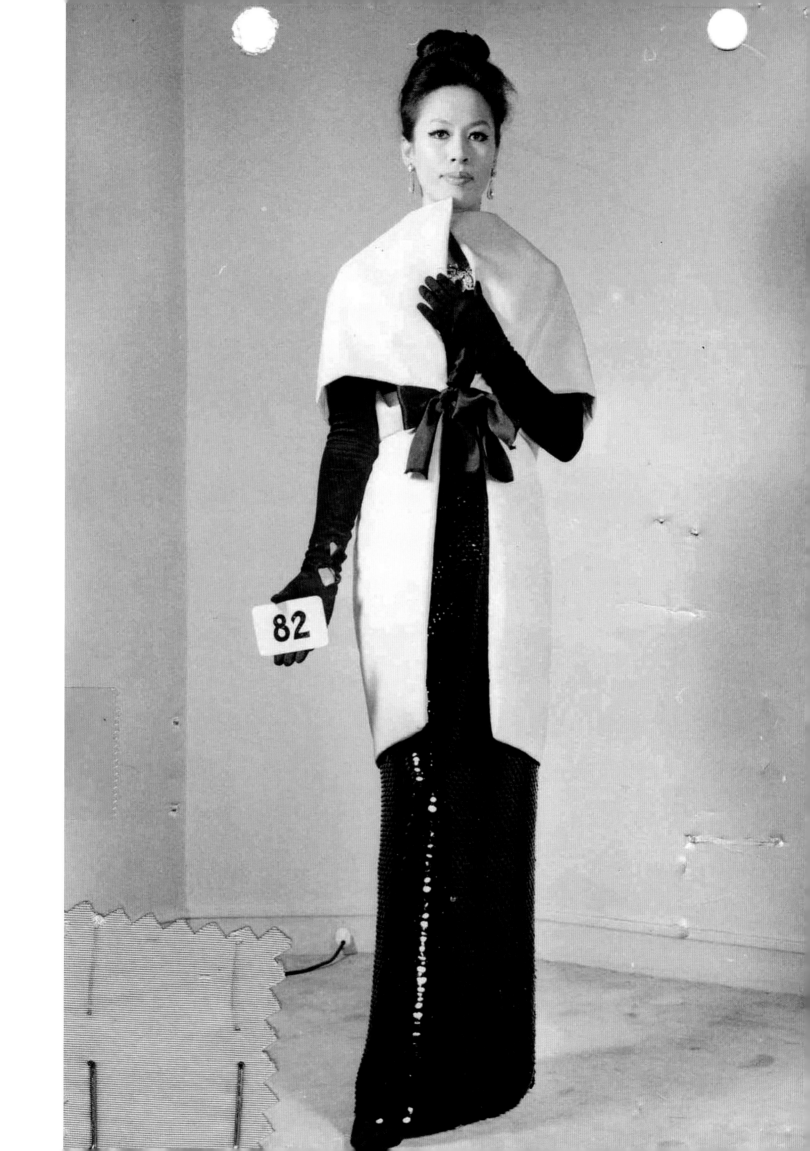

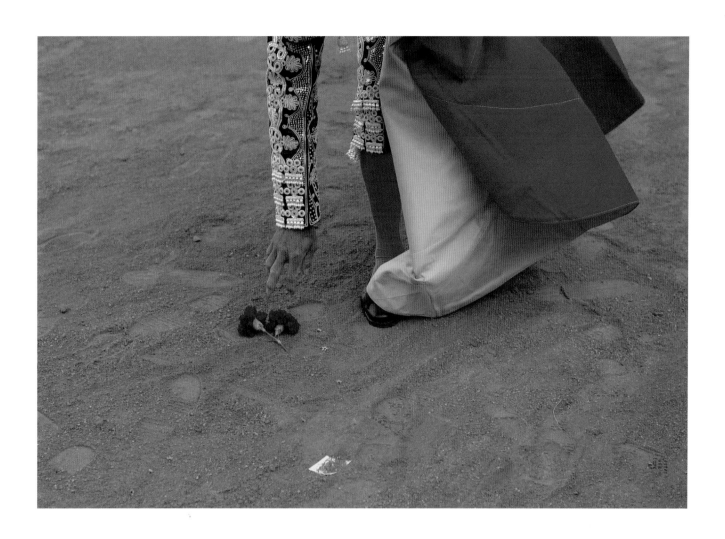

154
Cocktail dress of fuchsia silk shantung and black lace
with black silk satin ribbons, summer 1966
Fine Arts Museums of San Francisco, the Eleanor Christensen de Guigne Collection
(Mrs. Christian de Guigne III), gift of Ronna and Eric Hoffman

155
Matador picking up carnations in the Maestranza bullring, Seville, 2004

156
House photograph of evening dress of black silk damask
with carnation pattern and bright-pink silk corsage, winter 1957

157
Evening dress of white silk taffeta in a red carnation print with harem-style pouf skirt, summer 1956
Texas Fashion Collection, College of Visual Arts and Design,
University of North Texas, gift of Claudia de Osborne

158
John Rawlings
Cocktail hat of ivory silk satin, 1953
Originally published in *Vogue*, October 15, 1953

159
Matador Luis Miguel Dominguín, 1960

REGIONAL DRESS

Balenciaga traveled widely around his native Spain in the years before his move to Paris.[1] Following the establishment of his couture house in 1937, however, his trips to the country were generally limited to visiting his couture establishments in Madrid, Barcelona, and San Sebastián; his farmhouse at Monte Igueldo; and the spa town of Fitero in Navarra.[2] However, the memories of the Spanish regional dress that Balenciaga must have seen firsthand, along with examples of costumes and accessories in his collection, appear to have fed the designer's imagination. Thus, the Countess von Bismarck's coat of shaggy, hand-tufted Papacha mohair by Ascher (pl. 186) could have been fashioned for a Navarran shepherd (pl. 185); Princess Lilian of Belgium's draped toque hats evoke the headscarves of peasant women from La Montaña; and Diana Vreeland's loose blouses are similar to those worn by the fishermen of Guetaria.

Balenciaga's early career as a couturier in Spain coincided with an interest in Spanish folk traditions among anthropologists, costume historians, and artists who were anxious to document vanishing customs.[3] Balenciaga's friend Ignacio Zuloaga was in the vanguard of Spanish artists who had an interest in capturing folkloric dress on canvas (see pls. 133, 140, 169). A trip to Andalusia in 1882 had been an epiphany for Zuloaga, whose works thenceforth celebrated the lifestyle and costume of the region's Gypsies and the bravura style of the bullfighters.[4] As a young man, Balenciaga was undoubtedly familiar with Zuloaga's work. In 1921 the artist established a museum in Zumaia, a fishing village near Guetaria, where he displayed his own works alongside paintings in his collection by masters such as El Greco, Francisco de Zurbarán, and Francisco de Goya.[5] Balenciaga later dressed Zuloaga's French-born wife, Valentine Dethomas, and their daughter Lucía at his Spanish salons. Zuloaga even painted Lucía dressed by Balenciaga.[6]

The effects of folk dress that costume historian Miren Arzalluz has detected in Zuloaga's canvases—unnaturally stiffened ruffles and boldly flaring skirts—were attained through elaborate means.[7] Ruth Matilda Anderson, costume curator at the Hispanic Society of America, recalled the girls of Montehermoso wearing "six or seven pleated flannel petticoats" when dressing for "a rich wedding."[8] Their skirts were so vast that "a *montehermoseña* dressed to the nines can sit on a chair only by tilting it backward and perching on the edge."[9] Balenciaga, however, achieved similar silhouettes by using materials with extraordinary natural body, many of which were created specially for him.

In the 1910s the Guadalajaran José Ortiz-Echagüe began producing powerful and poetic photographs that similarly recorded aspects of local Spanish life and dress.[10] These iconic images were widely disseminated throughout Spain in the first half of the twentieth century, and it seems likely that Balenciaga would have been familiar with them.

In 1911 Archer M. Huntington, founder of the Hispanic Society of America, commissioned Joaquín Sorolla y Bastida to create a series of fourteen paintings depicting the provinces of Spain (see pls. 119, 135).[11] Finished in 1919, his magnificent canvases *Vision of Spain* reflect the artist's painstaking costume studies.[12] Anderson, whom Huntington dispatched to Spain in 1923 to record local dress traditions, scrupulously documented the painter's sources.[13] Traveling to some of the most remote parts of the country, she coaxed local men and women to wear their regional costumes—often reserved for festive occasions—for her

camera. Over four decades, Anderson "recorded a 'timeless Spain'" in more than fourteen thousand photographs, accompanied by notes that record the sitters' names and describe every detail of their dress.[14] It was a side of Spain that seemed to be fast disappearing; for instance, Anderson noted that an elaborate costume in La Alberca was one of only three still extant.[15]

Other regional-dress traditions proved more enduring. "In a large town or city where idlers are rude and uninhibited, a village person appearing in distinctive dress may have to suffer unwelcome attention or ridicule," wrote Anderson, but there were exceptions.[16] For example, nursemaids to the infants of the elite in turn-of-the-century Madrid were traditionally from Vega de Pas in Santander, the region neighboring Balenciaga's own.[17] They were readily identifiable by their dress, characterized by dark woolen skirts with plum-colored velvet bands of varying widths. Balenciaga used similar bands of scarlet and black velvet for a short, strapless evening dress from winter 1949. For the December 1949 cover of *Harper's Bazaar*, Richard Avedon photographed Dorian Leigh wearing it while flourishing a silver fan for added Spanish verisimilitude.

The photographs of Anderson and Ortiz-Echagüe are vital records of many of the sources that fed Balenciaga's creative process. Like the painters Zuloaga and Sorolla, the photographers followed in a documentary tradition that had existed since the eighteenth century. By that time each of the thirty-four Spanish provinces had begun to develop its unique costume, an evolution that would continue throughout the nineteenth century.[18] Albums of costume plates such as the *Colección de trajes de España* of 1777–1788 (see pls. 149, 180) brought the nuances of the nation's class and regional-dress differences to a wider European audience. Balenciaga had an extensive collection of historical women's magazines, and their fashion plates, as Marie-Andrée Jouve has discovered, often inspired his designs, particularly in the first decade of his Paris career.[19] During this period the silhouette, decoration, and accoutrements of fashionable dress from the third quarter of the nineteenth century appeared frequently in Balenciaga's work. "I found the clothes very pretty," wrote Bettina Ballard of his debut Paris collection, "particularly a group of long-sleeved, tight-bodiced at-home dresses that reminded me of *Little Women*."[20] Leonor Fini painted two such dresses from summer 1940 for *Harper's Bazaar* (pl. 163). The one on the right in particular evokes the sprigged cotton skirts seen in Miguel Viladrich Vilá's *Three Young Women of Fraga* (1904; pl. 162).

As Lesley Ellis Miller has pointed out, "the references to regional or peasant dress in Balenciaga's oeuvre overlap with those to costumes in paintings by old masters, because many of the regional garments were fossilized fashions of the past."[21] The headdress of a woman from Navarra, for example, retains a vestigial *liripipe* such as those portrayed by Albrecht Dürer and Ludger tom Ring the younger in the sixteenth century, a period similarly evoked in the shaped peplums of the velvet basques of Segovia.[22] Balenciaga adapted the *liripipe* hat in 1965 and interpreted the peplum detail in an embroidered satin ball-gown bodice from winter 1950 (pl. 78).

The caped cloaks worn by the elders of Ávila in Ortiz-Echagüe's 1916 photograph (pl. 184) are essentially unchanged from those worn by the *majos* in Goya's genre paintings of the late eighteenth and early nineteenth centuries.[23] In the 1950s *majo* cloaks were still available from fashionable tailors in Madrid such as Seseña, where the young Oscar de la Renta acquired one. In some areas of rural Spain, a bride's dowry included garments for her groom, such as "a long cape, which he wore at the wedding no matter how hot the weather."[24]

Balenciaga showed a group of cloaks in his winter 1948 collection, his use of silk faille and moiré adding an ecclesiastical tone (see pl. 183). Throughout his career he presented capes and cloaks in the manner in which they were worn in Spain. "If a Castillian is not born knowing how to wear this dramatic garment," Anderson recorded, "he begins at an early age learning to dominate it so that each fold will fall, to a hair-breadth, where he intends. Months are required for a new cape to become pliant and responsive to its master's hand. In order to arrange one with art, a man must give himself space enough to fling the material wide and high."[25] This dramatic gesture is suggested in Irving Penn's 1950 photograph of Régine d'Estribaud (pl. 61) in a dashing emerald-green stole.

It is tempting to speculate that Balenciaga must have been familiar with the Collección de trajes de España, especially when one compares, for example, his voluminous black taffeta evening coat from summer 1951 (pl. 173) with a plate depicting a citizen of Bilbao (pl. 172), whose own cape follows exactly the same line. At the same time, the extraordinary volume displayed in that coat, as well as in a pale oyster taffeta ball gown from summer 1952 (pl. 167) and a gray faille overskirt from winter 1956 (pl. 168), seems to represent the essence of mid-century fashion innovation. The latter ensemble also has a transformational aspect so beloved of Balenciaga—it is constructed to be worn as either a cape or an overskirt, a treatment that finds close parallel in the provinces of Ávila, Segovia, and Extremadura, where, as Anderson noted, "the habit of using the upper skirt as a cloak is common."[26]

In spite of their apparent modernity, however, these designs are closely related to the cobijada costumes of Vejer de la Frontera. Ortiz-Echagüe's photograph of three women in this costume (pl. 166) vividly suggests the era of Moorish rule in Andalusia (711–1492). Balenciaga interpreted this silhouette for a dress of black taffeta from winter 1950 (pl. 171). It seems conventional until one realizes that the skirt is bifurcated into enormous bloomers, like the bragas worn by Philip IV as a young man, which were a feature of masculine dress in León, Majorca, and Salamanca (see pl. 170) into the mid-twentieth century.[27]

Balenciaga's personal collection of costumes included Spanish folkloric pieces from which he drew inspiration.[28] One of these is a distinctive poke bonnet (gorra) from Montehermoso, made of braided natural straw with polychrome flannel, straw braid, buttons, and wool pom-pom trim. With its unusual high crown and duck-billed brim, it resembles an early-nineteenth-century bonnet, although in this region of Spain it was worn tipped forward at a jaunty angle over a dark, knotted headscarf. Anderson discovered the originator of these bonnets—Señora Maxima Hernández García—and praised the "inspired lunacy" of her creations.[29] She might well have been describing the fanciful hats concocted by Vladzio Zawrorowski d'Attainville, and later Ramón Esparza, to counterpoint the serious rigor of Balenciaga's ensembles (see pl. 211). The Montehermoso gorra recalls especially the shape of some of the wildly exaggerated hats created for Balenciaga by the Legroux sisters and by d'Attainville in Paris during the occupation.

Another important publication that might have influenced Balenciaga is the nineteenth-century Collection de costumes des diverses provinces de l'Espagne, which brought Spanish dress to a wider European audience at a time when Isabella II, her infantas, and aristocratic ladies were embracing a crinolined version of maja, or Sevillana, costume.[30] The furled skirt shown in one plate from the book (pl. 180), worn over a decorative petticoat, finds resonance in Balenciaga's peplums of the 1940s. He had experimented with fullness at the hip in the early years of the decade. Le Figaro noted "the bunched-up effect, washerwoman style" of his skirts for summer 1941.[31] The summer 1946 suit that was one

of the house's submissions to the Théâtre de la Mode—the Chambre Syndicale de la Couture's initiative to reinforce the continuing creativity and vitality of the Parisian haute couture in the wake of the occupation—featured a draped panel of fringed black faille forming the peplum of a fitted, hourglass-shaped black jacket over a softly flared skirt.[32] This suit presaged Christian Dior's Ligne Corolle, or "New Look," by a year.

Ortiz-Echagüe's portrait of a woman from Roncal (pl. 177), in Navarra, depicts her wearing her skirt furled up in front and falling almost to the hem of her petticoat in back, a silhouette that Balenciaga echoed very closely in a winter 1947 ensemble (pl. 178). Even the velvet bow he used suggests the Roncalesa's ribbon flourish in back. This gesture was prevalent throughout rural Spain and was the preferred method of self-presentation among fisherwomen. Raised in a fishing village, Balenciaga clearly had a natural respect for these women. Ballard remembered being introduced at Balenciaga's local fish market to "his best San Sebastián client—a raw-voiced fishwife with her skirts tucked up as she skidded around the slippery wet floors selling her fish. 'She orders all of my best models. She's the richest woman in town out of season,' he told me."[33]

For twenty years Balenciaga returned to sources of inspiration such as the elaborate cutwork embroideries of Salamanca; the splendid figured silks of Valencia; the full, pleated skirts of Extremadura and Ibiza; the flounced and ruffled skirts of Huelva and Andalusia; the basquinas of Aragon; and the fichus of Zamora and Valencia. During the wartime occupation, the transformational elements of regional dress, including fichus, overskirts with petticoats, overbodices, vests, and decorative aprons, could be called into service to cope with fabric restrictions and the need for a multifunctional wardrobe. For example, in one of its earliest postwar reports from Paris, Vogue illustrated Balenciaga's simple dinner dress of black wool and velvet from winter 1945, presented with a shawl of yellow taffeta embroidered with "bright flowers."[34] From the same period came a black wool jacket with a sumptuously embroidered double shawl collar (pl. 164); the woman in Viladrich Vilá's Catalans of Almatret (1915; pl. 165) wears a shawl embellished in much the same way that is draped across her bodice to create a similar effect.

In Balenciaga's later work, the clothing of his Basque homeland resonates most clearly.[35] His unfitted white cotton piqué blouse of 1953 (pl. 191) represented a radical departure from the hourglass silhouette that had dominated fashion since Dior launched his New Look in 1947. The blouse evoked the utilitarian sailor shirts and fishermen's blouses that Balenciaga would have seen in Guetaria as well as those worn by local peasants even on festive occasions.[36] Balenciaga continued to explore the idea of these smocks as an important element in the sophisticated woman's wardrobe (see pl. 190).

In the late nineteenth century, the Basques were known for some of the most extreme mourning dress in Europe.[37] Black was the color of Balenciaga's childhood. His father died in 1906, and subsequently the women of his family dressed in this traditional color of mourning. Black, in all its tones, was a motif of Balenciaga's work throughout his career, allowing him to accentuate the silhouette of his bravura innovations. So, too, were the brilliant yellow (Vogue noted an "intense Seville yellow") and red of the Spanish flag.[38] This is a color combination so inherent in the Spanish identity that the throne room at the Royal Palace in Madrid (pl. 193) is decorated in this scheme.

The Basque beret, the traditional headgear of the region's shepherds, was a hat type that inspired Balenciaga throughout the 1960s. In Ortiz-Echagüe's painterly study of the tavern in Orio (pl. 187), the innkeeper's wife wears her hair bound in a scarf that is knotted in the back. Balenciaga imitated this treatment, sometimes with the silk foulard scarves designed and printed for him by Sache, by building up the scarf over a domed hat form. The dour innkeeper wears his beret with a simple and practical loose-fitting shirt jacket. In its wide neckline, deep-set sleeves, and square-cut shape it recalls the suits and tunics in which Balenciaga dressed the most sophisticated women of the 1960s (see pls. 188, 190). In addition to reinterpreting the varied traditional dress of many of Spain's regions, Balenciaga revolutionized fashion by referencing the sturdy, utilitarian garments worn by the Spanish laboring classes—as well as the attitude and philosophy that shaped them—to create a new paradigm of mid-century elegance.

161
Studio sketch of evening gown of black tulle with satin cuir
and sequin embroidery by Ginisty and Quenolle, winter 1951

162
Miguel Viladrich Vilá
Three Young Women of Fraga, 1904, oil on panel
The Hispanic Society of America, New York

163
Leonor Fini
From left: dinner dress of black silk jersey with jet flowers;
dress of brown cotton sprigged with moss roses, summer 1940
Originally published in *Harper's Bazaar*, May 1940

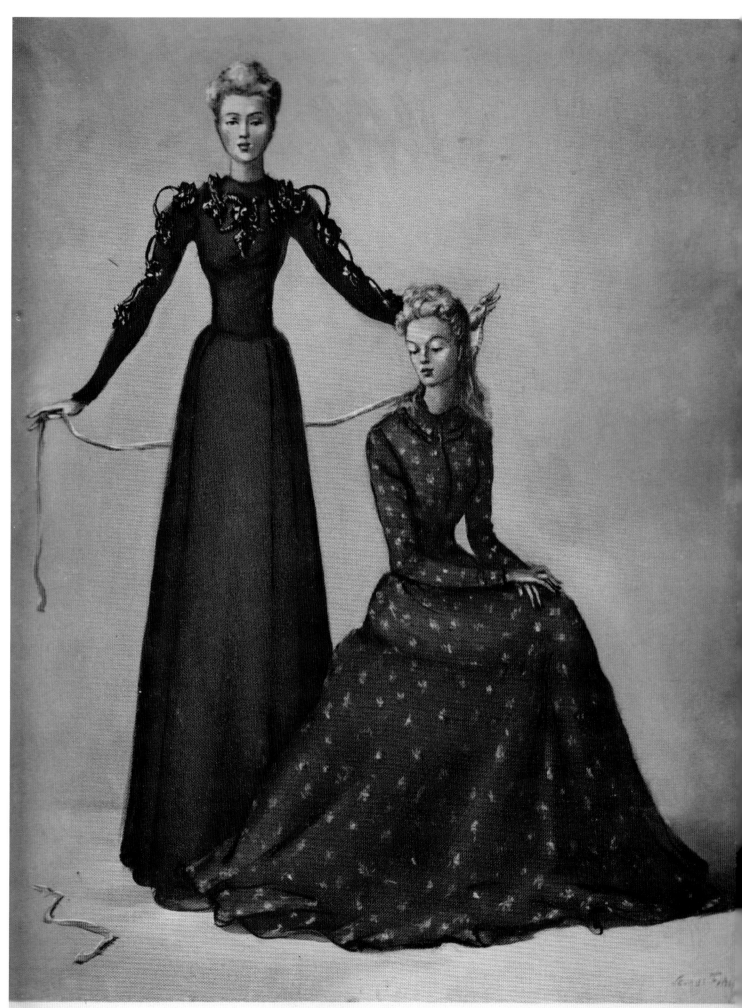

Contrasts by Balenciaga

164
Bolero of black crepe, metallic thread, and paillettes, ca. 1945
Archives Balenciaga, Paris

165
Miguel Viladrich Vilá
Catalans of Almatret, 1915, oil on panel
The Hispanic Society of America, New York

166
José Ortiz-Echagüe
Vejer—Three Cobijadas, 1926

167
Karen Radkai
Evening gown of oyster silk taffeta and black lace, summer 1952
Originally published in *Harper's Bazaar*, March 1952

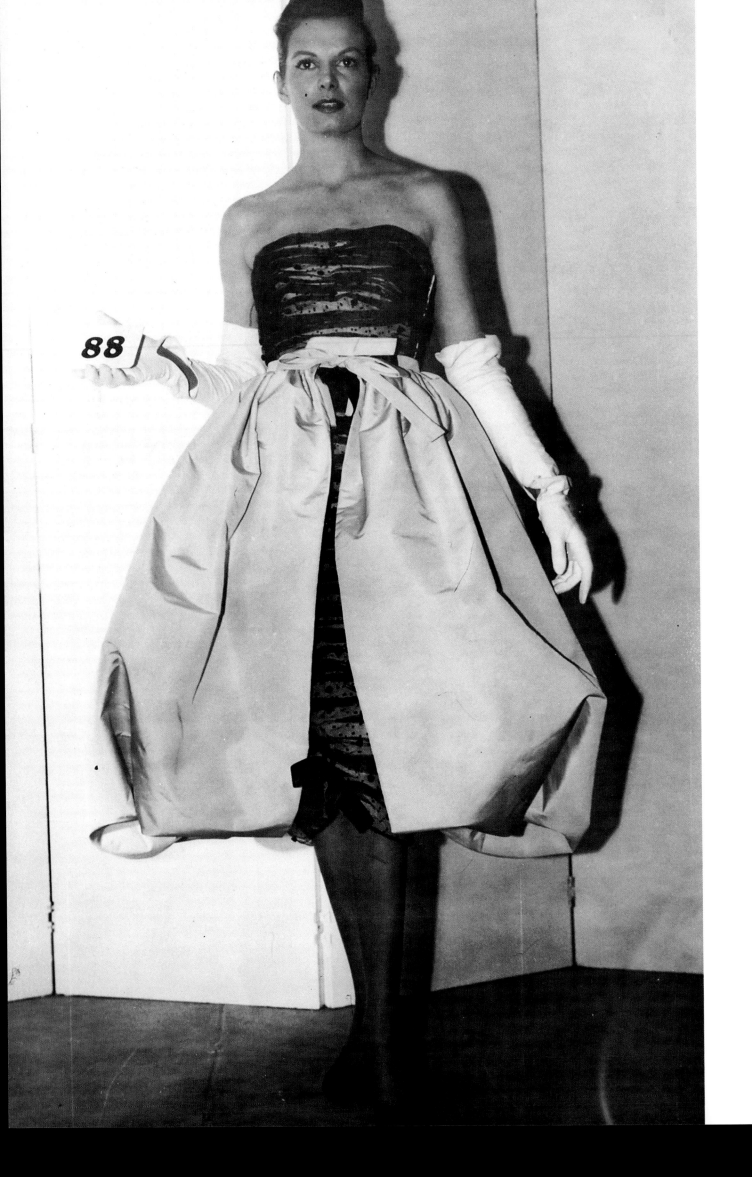

168
House photograph of evening dress of black point d'esprit with overskirt of gray silk faille, winter 1956

169
Ignacio Zuloaga
Women of Sepúlveda, 1909, oil on canvas
Ayunamiento de Irún, Spain

170
José Ortiz-Echagüe
Festival Dress in Villarino—Salamanca, ca. 1950

171
House photograph of evening dress of black silk taffeta, winter 1950

D. Luis Paret del.

D. Juan de la Cruz sc.

Ciudadana de Bilbao. | Bourgeoise de Bilbao.

172
"Citizen of Bilbao," plate 52 in Juan de la Cruz Cano y Olmedilla, *Colección de trajes de España*, 1777–1788
The Hispanic Society of America, New York

173
House photograph of evening cape of black silk taffeta, summer 1951

174
José Ortiz-Echagüe
Salamanca—Peñaparda—Water Carriers, early 20th century

175
Studio sketch of afternoon suit of black silk satin matelassé, winter 1950

202

Claude 53 Marie

Tessues Raimon

176
Richard Avedon
Dovima wearing suit of black silk satin matelassé, winter 1950
Variant originally published in *Harper's Bazaar*, October 1950

177
José Ortiz-Echagüe
Roncalesa, 1916–1930

178
Day dress of black silk bengaline and velvet, winter 1947
Fine Arts Museums of San Francisco, gift of Mrs. Eloise Heidland

Pigal.

Lith de Langlumé

Femme des environs du Pardo ↕ *Muger de las cercanias del Pardo*

179
House photograph of dinner dress of black silk satin with white chiné polka dots, winter 1953

180
"Woman from near Pardo," plate 88 in Pigal,
Collection de costumes des diverses provinces de l'Espagne, ca. 1830
The Hispanic Society of America, New York

181
Salamancan skirt of cutwork embroidery, late 19th century
Museo del Traje, Madrid

182
Dress of black wool and pink silk taffeta, winter 1948
Phoenix Art Museum, gift of Peggy Eliasberg

183
Clifford Coffin
Wenda Parkinson wearing evening coat of black silk faille, winter 1948
Originally published in *Vogue*, September 15, 1948

184
José Ortiz-Echagüe
Escopeta, Vinazo y Centeno, 1916

185
Navarran shepherd, 1925

186
House photograph of coat of Papacha mohair by Ascher, winter 1965

187
José Ortiz-Echagüe
Tavern in Orio, ca. 1932

188
Day suit of olive wool, winter 1962
Fine Arts Museums of San Francisco, the Eleanor Christensen de Guigne Collection
(Mrs. Christian de Guigne III), gift of Ronna and Eric Hoffman

189
Studio drawing of coat of black wool, winter 1967

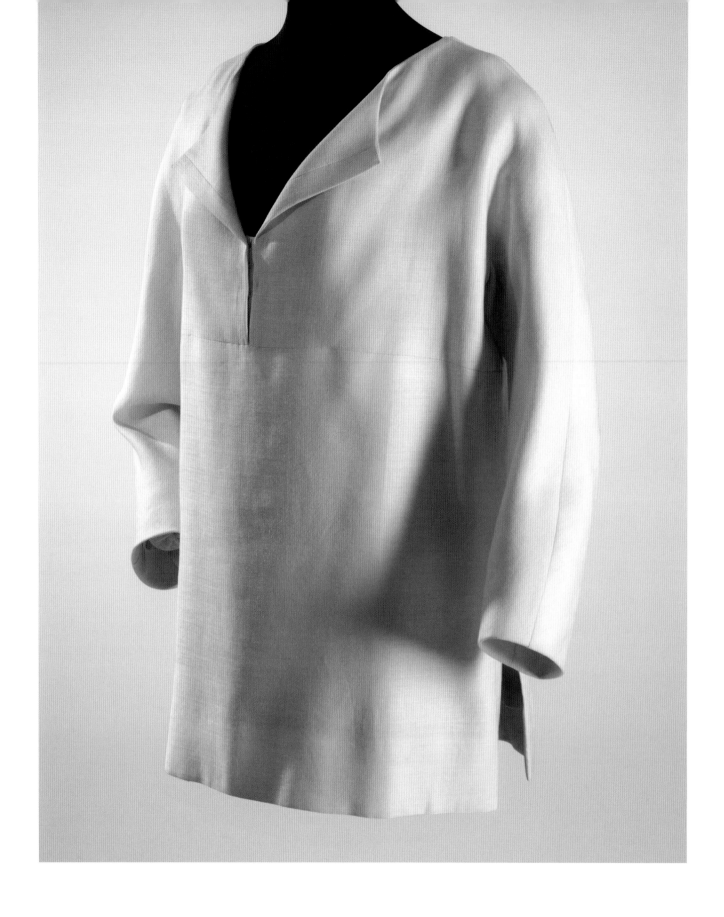

190
Tunic of ivory linen, summer 1964
The Museum at the Fashion Institute of Technology, New York, gift of Givenchy, Inc.

191
Louise Dahl-Wolfe
Suzy Parker by the Seine wearing tunic of white cotton piqué, summer 1953
Originally published in *Harper's Bazaar*, March 1953

192
Horst P. Horst
Suit of red linen, summer 1952
Originally published in *Vogue*, March 1952

193
Throne room in the Royal Palace, Madrid

194
Jean Patchett wearing suit of mustard-yellow linen, summer 1950
British *Vogue*, April 1950

195
Suit of mustard-yellow linen, summer 1950
Collection of Hamish Bowles

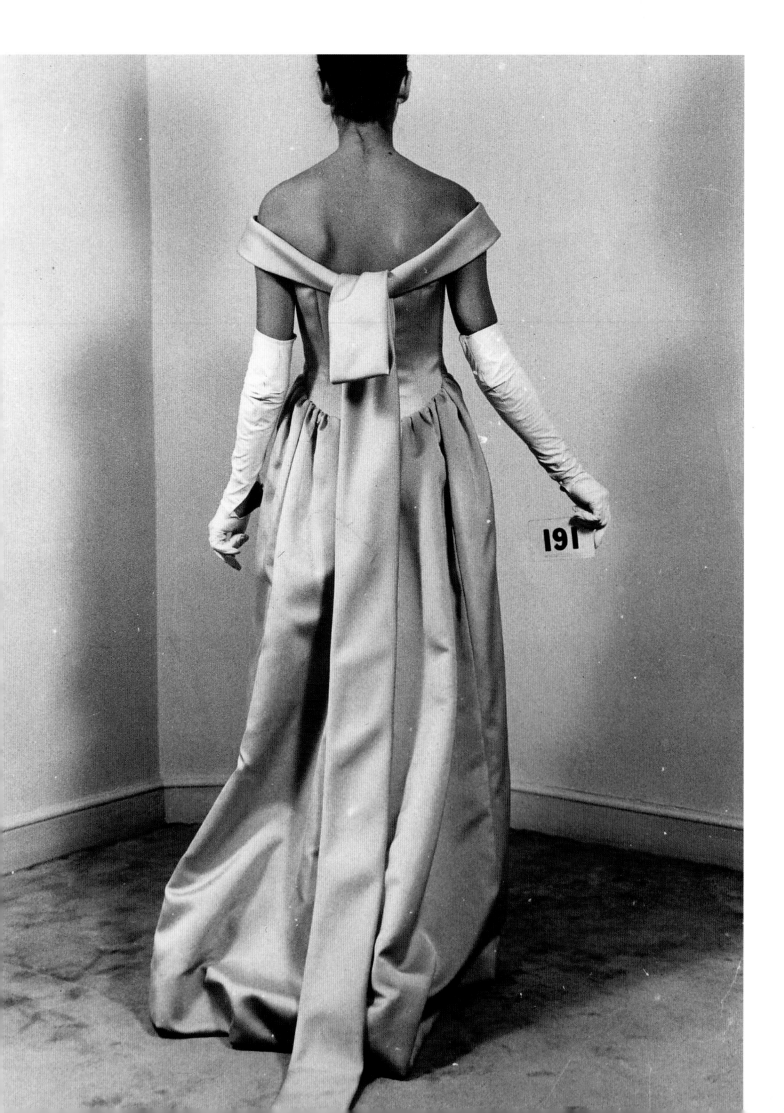

196
House photograph of evening gown of yellow silk satin, winter 1962

197
Studio sketch of evening dress of yellow lace, summer 1957

198
Studio sketch of evening dress of red lace, summer 1957

199
Studio sketch of evening dress of yellow silk linen, winter 1961

200
Studio sketch of evening dress of red silk-satin organza, summer 1957

201
House photograph of evening dress of cerise silk faille, winter 1954

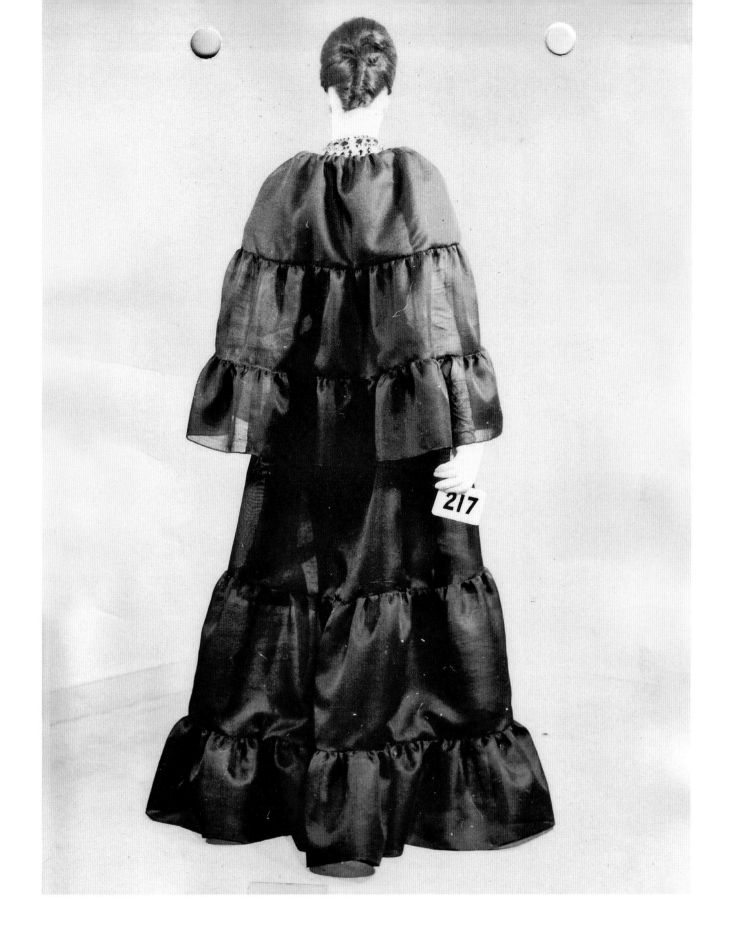

202
Juan Bautista Martínez del Mazo
Infanta Margarita Teresa of Spain in Mourning Dress, 1666, oil on canvas
Museo Nacional del Prado, Madrid

203
House photograph of evening ensemble with dress and cape of black silk gauze, summer 1964

204
Studio drawing of day dress of black wool jersey, winter 1957

205
Studio drawing of cocktail ensemble with dress and bloomers of black silk dotted organdy, summer 1959

206
House photograph of cocktail dress of black silk shantung, summer 1958

156

207
Evening dress of black crepe, 1940
Archives Balenciaga, Paris

208
House photograph of evening dress of black silk crepe, winter 1967

Balenciaga ruffles—wanted by the woman who's never had a ruffled thought in her head. Evening suit, in a stiffish black marquisette; the jacket ruffles shaped, at front, into the jutting peplum effect that Balenciaga showed this year; the skirt, longer, more deeply ruffled at back, almost stately. In America, at I. Magnin.

VOGUE, APRIL 15, 1962

95

209
Tod Draz
Evening ensemble of black silk gazar, summer 1962
Originally published in *Vogue*, April 15, 1962

210
Tom Kublin
Evening ensemble of black silk gazar, winter 1964
Originally published in *Harper's Bazaar*, December 1964

211 (following spread)
Cocktail hat of black silk organza, 1961
The Museum at the Fashion Institute of Technology, New York, gift of Helen Gettier

Mrs. Loel Guinness

Right:
On the second floor,
10 Avenue Georges Cinq,
Mrs. Guinness, standing before the
little gold chairs of his salon,
in Balenciaga's superb black
evening dress of silk
gazar. The deep back décolletage,
swept, as if by wings, in a short,
tiered cape. Coiffure by Christian.

Chez Balenciaga

Opposite: Mrs. Guinness,
her profile, like her white satin
toque, a delicate, modern
rendering of Nefertiti. The
Balenciaga cape-coat she wears over a
short evening dress, black wool
lace encircled from throat
to hem in a thick encrusting of
sparkling jets and tiny
cellophane balls,
glistening overall with threads
of black cellophane.

KUBLIN

NOTES

INTRODUCTION

1. Prudence Glynn, "Balenciaga and *la Vie d'un Chien*," *Times* (London), August 3, 1971, 6.
2. Christian Dior, quoted in Marie-France Pochna, *Christian Dior* (New York: Overlook Press, 2008), 88.
3. Christian Dior, quoted in Marie-Andrée Jouve and Jacqueline Demornex, *Balenciaga* (New York: Rizzoli, 1989), 58.
4. Pamela Golbin, *Balenciaga Paris* (London: Thames and Hudson, 2006), 21.
5. Diana Vreeland, *D.V.* (London: Weidenfeld and Nicolson, 1984), 106.
6. Carmel Snow with Mary Louise Aswell, *The World of Carmel Snow* (New York: McGraw-Hill, 1962), 165.
7. Colin McDowell, "Hommage à Balenciaga," *Country Life*, October 17, 1985.
8. *Harper's Bazaar*, October 1938, 69.
9. Bettina Ballard, *In My Fashion* (New York: David McKay, 1960), 116.
10. José María de Areilza, "The Image of Cristóbal Balenciaga," in *El mundo de Balenciaga: Palacio de Bibliotecas y Museos, Salas de la Dirección General de Bellas Artes* (Barcelona: Productoras Nacionales de Fibras Artificiales y Sintéticas, 1974), 24-25.
11. Ballard, *In My Fashion*, 107, describes Balenciaga's dislike of bullfights.
12. This was true even as late as 1972, when ladies in attendance at the wedding of General Franco's granddaughter María Carmen Martínez Bordiú y Franco wore the black lace mantilla, along with the high, carved-horn combs introduced in the early nineteenth century. Balenciaga came out of retirement to create the bride's dress.
13. *Harper's Bazaar*, September 15, 1939, 64.
14. *Les chefs-d'oeuvres du Musée du Prado* (Geneva: Musée d'Art et d'Histoire, 1939), 5-6.
15. "Exhibit in Geneva Authorized by Franco Government," *New York Times*, April 21, 1939.
16. Notable among the couturiers influenced by the exhibition was Balenciaga's friend and fellow Spaniard Ana de Pombo, then designer for the house of Paquin.
17. Clair Price, "Stirring Odyssey of Spanish Art," *New York Times*, May 28, 1939.
18. Snow and Aswell, *World of Carmel Snow*, 136.
19. Cecil Beaton, *The Glass of Fashion* (London: Weidenfeld and Nicolson, 1954), 259.
20. Sebastian Balfour, "Spain from 1931 to the Present," in *Spain: A History* (Oxford: Oxford University Press, 2000), 260.
21. Richard Martin, "Balenciaga," *American Fabrics and Fashions*, September-October 1986, 25.
22. "Behind Him and within Him—Lies Spain," *Life*, December 27, 1968, 30.
23. Maria M. Delgado, *Federico García Lorca* (New York: Routledge, 2008), 16.
24. Lynn Garafola, *Diaghilev's Ballets Russes* (Cambridge, MA: Da Capo Press, 1998), 88.
25. Balfour, "Spain," 264-273.
26. Eva Duarte Perón held an exhibition of her own collection of Spanish national dress at the Museo Nacional de Arte Decorativo in Buenos Aires in 1948. Presumably this collection had been acquired on her 1947 Rainbow Tour of Europe that included a visit to General Franco, who gave her Spain's highest government award, the Order of Isabella the Catholic.
27. See José Ortiz-Echagüe, *España: Tipos y Trajes* (Bilbao: Décima Edición, 1957).
28. As fashion historian Aileen Ribeiro has noted, these garments even recall those worn by Albrecht Dürer's bourgeois German women at the turn of the sixteenth century. This costume was introduced to the Spanish court by the Hapsburg monarchs. Aileen Ribeiro, "Fashioning the Feminine: Dress in Goya's Portraits of Women," in *Goya: Images of Women*, ed. Janis A. Tomlinson (Washington, DC: National Gallery of Art, 2002), 77-81.
29. *Harper's Bazaar*, July 1962, 82.
30. Hubert de Givenchy, interview with author, June 2010.
31. For a glossary of bullfighting terms, see *Los Toros: Bullfighting* (Madrid: Indice, 1964), 7-13.
32. Agustín Balenciaga Medina, interview with author, September 2010.
33. Gustave Zumsteg, quoted in Golbin, *Balenciaga Paris*, 151.
34. Judith Thurman, "The Absolutist: Cristóbal Balenciaga's Cult of Perfection," *New Yorker*, July 3, 2006, 62.
35. "Balenciaga—and the Art of Making Elegant Clothes," *Women's Wear Daily*, July 9, 1958, 26.
36. British *Vogue* (1962), quoted in Golbin, *Balenciaga Paris*, 127.
37. "Balenciaga—and the Art of Making Elegant Clothes," 26.
38. Myra Walker, interview with author, September 2010.
39. Gabrielle "Coco" Chanel, quoted in Gloria Emerson, "Balenciaga, the Couturier, Dead at 77," *New York Times*, March 23, 1972.
40. Ballard, *In My Fashion*, 110.
41. "Balenciaga—and the Art of Making Elegant Clothes," 26.
42. Diana Vreeland, "Balenciaga: An Appreciation," in *The World of Balenciaga* (New York: Metropolitan Museum of Art, 1973), 9.
43. *Harper's Bazaar*, September 1948, 178.
44. Gloria Guinness, "Cristóbal Balenciaga," in *World of Balenciaga*, 16.
45. Snow and Aswell, *World of Carmel Snow*, 167.
46. Hamish Bowles, "The Balenciaga Mystique," *Vogue*, March 2006, 516.
47. Guinness, "Cristóbal Balenciaga," 16.
48. Bowles, "Balenciaga Mystique," 512.
49. Kennedy Fraiser, "On and Off the Avenue: Feminine Fashions," *New Yorker*, June 16, 1973, 89.
50. Pauline de Rothschild, "Balenciaga," in *World of Balenciaga*, 23.
51. Ballard, *In My Fashion*, 117.
52. Beaton, *Glass of Fashion*, 266.
53. Erica Billeter, "Cristóbal Balenciaga, Fashion King in a Museum," *Annabelle*, July 1, 1970, 11.
54. Susan Train, interview with author, January 2010.
55. Guinness, "Cristóbal Balenciaga," 15.
56. Vreeland, *D.V.*, 106.
57. Margaret Thompson Biddle, "The Art of Dressing Well," *Woman's Home Companion*, November 1953, quoted in *Current Biography: Who's News and Why*, ed. M. Dent Candee (New York: H. W. Wilson, 1954), 66.
58. *Women's Wear Daily*, quoted in Ballard, *In My Fashion*, 115.
59. Snow and Aswell, *World of Carmel Snow*, 167.
60. Rothschild, "Balenciaga," 18; and "Appreciation," reproduced in this volume, 7-12.
61. Golbin, *Balenciaga Paris*, 152.
62. Cristóbal Balenciaga, quoted in Glynn, "Balenciaga," 6.
63. "The Little Black Dress," *Harper's Bazaar*, September 15, 1938, 71.
64. The disagreement arose after Chanel promised *WWD* a portrait of Balenciaga and herself without consulting him. Balenciaga's dislike of the press bordered on the pathological. When he refused to sit for the photograph, Chanel gave the newspaper an interview in which she criticized him as out of touch and essentially antipathetic to women. It was an accusation she was inclined to level at the male couturiers who, to her uncontained fury, came to dominate the haute couture after the war.
65. Colin McDowell, "Balenciaga: The Quiet Revolutionary," British *Vogue*, July 1989, 135.
66. Ballard, *In My Fashion*, 116.
67. Cristóbal Balenciaga, quoted in "Balenciaga—and the Art of Making Elegant Clothes," 26.
68. Bunny Mellon, letter to author, June 28, 2010.
69. Ernestine Carter, *Magic Names of Fashion* (Englewood Cliffs, NJ: Prentice-Hall, 1980), 11.
70. Givenchy, interview with author, June 2010.
71. José Balenciaga Basurto resigned as mayor after a short period, following disagreements with his fellow councillors.
72. Jouve and Demornex, *Balenciaga*, 17.
73. Ballard, *In My Fashion*, 108.
74. Rothschild, "Balenciaga," 18.
75. Ibid.
76. Balenciaga Medina, interview with author.
77. Lesley Ellis Miller, *Balenciaga* (London: V&A Publications, 2007), 22.
78. Ibid.
79. Balenciaga Medina, interview with author.
80. As Pauline de Rothschild notes in her "Appreciation," the scale of the Church of San Salvador is disproportionate to the medieval houses that surround it.
81. Hubert de Givenchy, quoted in Elsa Klensch, "Balenciaga: Fashion Changer," *Vogue*, May 1973, 150.
82. *San Sebastián, Spain* (New York: International Telephone and Telegraph Corporation, Bureau of Information Pro-España), 7.
83. Bowles, "Balenciaga Mystique," 514.
84. Rothschild, "Balenciaga," 19; and "Appreciation," this volume.
85. Vreeland, *D.V.*, 107.
86. Jouve and Demornex, *Balenciaga*, 17-20.
87. Miller, *Balenciaga*, 24.
88. *San Sebastián, Spain*, 3.
89. Miller, *Balenciaga*, 22.
90. Igor Uria Zubizarreta, interview with author, January 2006. The suit is in the collection of the Fundación Cristóbal Balenciaga in Guetaria, Spain.
91. *Vogue* (1963), quoted in Golbin, *Balenciaga Paris*, 129.
92. Jouve and Demornex, *Balenciaga*, 23, 31.
93. Cristóbal Balenciaga, quoted in *Harper's Bazaar*, October 1, 1967, 135.
94. Jouve and Demornex, *Balenciaga*, 31.
95. Palmer White, *Elsa Schiaparelli: Empress of Paris Fashion* (New York: Rizzoli, 1986), 216.
96. Beaton, *Glass of Fashion*, 265.

97. Glynn, "Balenciaga," 6.

98. Gerard Noel, *Ena: Spain's English Queen* (London: Constable, 1984), 122.

99. Feliza Salvagnac, quoted in Billeter, "Cristóbal Balenciaga," 11.

100. McDowell, "Quiet Revolutionary," 135.

101. Golbin, *Balenciaga Paris*, 31, states that following the bankruptcy of the firm Cristóbalbalenciaga, the company reopened branches in San Sebastián, Madrid, and Barcelona under the name Eisa between 1932 and 1936.

102. Myra Walker, *Balenciaga and His Legacy* (New Haven, CT: Yale University Press, 2006), 13-14.

103. McDowell, "Quiet Revolutionary," 135. Hartnell had moved closer to the British throne by designing the dress for Lady Alice Christabel Montague Douglas Scott's 1935 wedding to the king's brother Prince Henry, the Duke of Gloucester, and for her bridesmaids, the royal princesses Elizabeth and Margaret Rose.

104. Jouve and Demornex, *Balenciaga*, 31.

105. Snow and Aswell, *World of Carmel Snow*, 165.

106. Mainbocher's star was then in its ascendancy, as he has created the wedding dress for Wallis Warfield Simpson's wedding to the Duke of Windsor on June 3 of that year.

107. Golbin, *Balenciaga Paris*, 61.

108. Billeter, "Cristóbal Balenciaga," 13.

109. Rosamond Bernier, interview with author, June 2010.

110. Deeda Blair and Jerry Silverman, quoted in "They Remember Balenciaga," *Women's Wear Daily*, March 27, 1972, 16.

111. Carter, *Magic Names of Fashion*, 106-107.

112. Percy Savage, "Balenciaga the Great," *Observer* (London), October 13, 1985, 51.

113. Ballard, *In My Fashion*, 118.

114. Chez Christian Dior, models twirling their full skirts frequently upset the tall ashtray stands that were dotted around the salons for the benefit of the clients. Train, interview with author.

115. Bernier, interview with author.

116. Beaton, *Glass of Fashion*, 264.

117. *Harper's Bazaar*, September 15, 1938, 71.

118. Ibid.

119. Diana Vreeland, quoted in Klensch, "Balenciaga: Fashion Changer," 150.

120. Snow and Aswell, *World of Carmel Snow*, 125.

121. Golbin, *Balenciaga Paris*, 36.

122. *Harper's Bazaar*, February 1938, 34.

123. *Harper's Bazaar*, April 1940, 61.

124. Ibid.

125. Jouve and Demornex, *Balenciaga*, 46.

126. Patrick O'Higgins, *Madame: An Intimate Biography of Helena Rubinstein* (New York: Viking Press, 1971), 133.

127. Beaton, *Glass of Fashion*, 263.

128. Anny Latour, *Kings of Fashion*, trans. Mervyn Savill (New York: Coward-McCann, 1958), 260.

129. In 1948, Ramón Esparza became his personal assistant. Fernando Martínez Herreros, his secretary, joined in 1950. Miller, *Balenciaga*, 30.

130. Biddle, "Art of Dressing Well," quoted in Candee, *Current Biography*, 66.

131. Pochna, *Christian Dior*, 87.

132. Cristóbal Balenciaga, quoted in Glynn, "Balenciaga," 6.

133. Dominique Veillon, *Fashion under the Occupation*, trans. Miriam Kochan (Oxford: Berg, 2002), 99.

134. Pochna, *Christian Dior*, 88.

135. Guinness, "Cristóbal Balenciaga," 16.

136. *Harper's Bazaar*, March 1944, 98.

137. Cristóbal Balenciaga, quoted in *Harper's Bazaar*, October 1946, 224.

138. Christian Dior, *Dior by Dior*, trans. Antonia Fraser (Middlesex, UK: Penguin Books, 1958), 11-25.

139. Train, interview with author.

140. Charlotte Mosley, ed., *The Letters of Nancy Mitford: Love from Nancy* (Boston: Houghton Mifflin, 1993), 180-181.

141. Ballard, *In My Fashion*, 116.

142. Pochna, *Christian Dior*, 69.

143. Ibid., 192.

144. Ibid., 191.

145. Carter, *Magic Names of Fashion*, 101.

146. Ballard, *In My Fashion*, 114.

147. Christian Dior, quoted in "The King Is Dead," *Women's Wear Daily*, March 27, 1972, 5.

148. *Harper's Bazaar*, quoted in Golbin, *Balenciaga Paris*, 67.

149. Givenchy, interview with author.

150. Ballard, *In My Fashion*, 114.

151. Guinness, "Cristóbal Balenciaga," 16.

152. Beaton, *Glass of Fashion*, 262.

153. Ballard, *In My Fashion*, 112.

154. "Balenciaga—and the Art of Making Elegant Clothes," 26.

155. Ballard, *In My Fashion*, 104.

156. Snow and Aswell, *World of Carmel Snow*, 165.

157. Billeter, "Cristóbal Balenciaga," 13.

158. Feliza Salvagnac, quoted in ibid., 10.

159. Bowles, "Balenciaga Mystique," 514.

160. Thurman, "Absolutist," 59.

161. Jouve and Demornex, *Balenciaga*, 84.

162. Cordelia Biddle Robertson, "Notes from Spain," *Vogue*, June 1950, 80.

163. Régine d'Estribaud, interview with author, September 2010.

164. Golbin, *Balenciaga Paris*, 24.

165. Bernier, interview with author.

166. Feliza Salvagnac, quoted in Billeter, "Cristóbal Balenciaga," 13.

167. Guinness, "Cristóbal Balenciaga."

168. Sonsoles Diez de Rivera, interview with author, January 2006.

169. Ballard, *In My Fashion*, 109.

170. Beaton, *Glass of Fashion*, 267.

171. Vreeland, *D.V.*, 106.

172. Bernier, interview with author.

173. Ashley Hicks, *David Hicks: A Life of Design* (New York: Rizzoli, 2008), 62.

174. Deeda Blair, interview with author, June 2010.

175. Doris Brynner, interview with author, September 2010.

176. Bernier, interview with author.

177. Ballard, *In My Fashion*, 104.

178. Emerson, "Balenciaga, the Couturier."

179. Glynn, "Balenciaga," 6.

180. Cristóbal Balenciaga, quoted in Golbin, *Balenciaga Paris*, 151.

181. Givenchy, interview with author.

182. Cristóbal Balenciaga, quoted in Ballard, *In My Fashion*, 119.

183. Valérie Guillaume, *Courrèges*, trans. Lorna Dale (New York: Assouline, 2004), 6.

184. Father Robert Pieplu, "Eulogy for Balenciaga," in *World of Balenciaga*, 12.

185. White, *Elsa Schiaparelli*, 216.

186. Diana Vreeland, quoted in Klensch, "Balenciaga: Fashion Changer," 150.

187. Rothschild, "Balenciaga," 24; and "Appreciation," this volume.

188. Cristóbal Balenciaga, quoted in Glynn, "Balenciaga," 6.

189. "The King Is Dead," 4.

190. Elizabeth Wilson, *Adorned in Dreams: Fashion and Modernity* (Piscataway, NJ: Rutgers University Press, 2003), 174.

191. Givenchy, interview with author.

192. Virginie Merlin-Teysserre, quoted in Golbin, *Balenciaga Paris*, 151.

193. Cristóbal Balenciaga, quoted in Glynn, "Balenciaga," 6.

194. Virginie Merlin-Teysserre, quoting Balenciaga, in Golbin, *Balenciaga Paris*, 151.

195. Jouve and Demornex, *Balenciaga*, 130.

196. Golbin, *Balenciaga Paris*, 151.

197. Vreeland, *D.V.*, 107.

198. "El album de la boda: Carmen y Alfonso," *Gaceta Illustrada*, March 1972.

199. María del Carmen Martínez-Bordiú y Franco, quoted in Bernadine Morris, "Salute to the Art of Balenciaga," *New York Times*, October 1, 1985.

200. Ballard, *In My Fashion*, 112-113.

201. Givenchy, interview with author. Mitzah Bricard was an erstwhile muse and milliner to Edward Molyneux and, subsequently, to Christian Dior. Her elegance was legendary.

202. Ibid.

203. Patricia McColl, "We Are All His Family," *Women's Wear Daily*, March 27, 1972, 32.

204. *San Sebastián, Spain*, 7.

205. "The King Is Dead," 4-5.

SPANISH ART

1. Billeter, "Cristóbal Balenciaga," 8.

2. Glynn, "Balenciaga," 6.

3. Ballard, *In My Fashion*, 112.

4. Jouve and Demornex, *Balenciaga*, 99.

5. *Les chefs d'oeuvres du Musée du Prado*, 5-6.

6. *Harper's Bazaar*, September 1, 1939, 49.

7. Alan S. Cole, "The Art of Lace-Making," *Journal of the Society of Arts* 29 (September 9, 1881): 774.

8. Jouve and Demornex, *Balenciaga*, 320-321.

9. Ibid., 309.

10. C. Gasquoine Hartley, *A Record of Spanish Painting* (London: Walter Scott, 1904), 174-175.

11. Patrick Lenaghan, ed., *The Hispanic Society of America: Tesoros* (New York: Hispanic Society of America, 2000), 278.

12. Ribeiro, "Fashioning the Feminine," 84.

13. "Mrs. Byron C. Foy, A Society Leader," *New York Times*, August 21, 1957.

14. Ballard, *In My Fashion*, 116-117.

15. Ibid.

16. Robert Hughes, *Goya* (New York: Knopf, 2006), 164.

17. Ibid.

18. Ibid., 81.

19. Ribeiro, "Fashioning the Feminine," 74.

20. Ibid., 82.

21. Bury Palliser, *A History of Lace* (London: Sampson Low, Marston, 1865), 89.

22. Alexandre Laborde, quoted in Ribeiro, "Fashioning the Feminine," 83.
23. Gloria Emerson, "Monarch of Haute Couture: Balenciaga the Unsurpassed," *New York Times*, August 5, 1967.
24. McDowell, "Hommage à Balenciaga."
25. Beaton, *Glass of Fashion*, 259.
26. Martin, "Balenciaga," 25–26.
27. Percy Savage, interviewed by Linda Sandino, in "National Life Stories: An Oral History of British Fashion," British Library Sound Archive, London, 2004, C1046/09, 58–59.
28. Jouve and Demornex, *Balenciaga*, 99.
29. *Hommage to Balenciaga* (1990) by Eduardo Chillida is in the collection of the Museo Chillida-Leku near San Sebastián.

ROYAL COURT

1. Ruth Matilda Anderson, *Hispanic Costume: 1480–1530* (New York: Hispanic Society of America, 1979), 245. Fifteenth-century panels, such as *Saint Blaise Curing a Child* from Villalonquéjar, document the use of ermine in dress.
2. Ibid., 201, 245. Balenciaga had used ermine tails playfully before, as on the epaulets of an early-1940s evening coat.
3. "El album de la boda."
4. Henry Kamen, "Spain's Dominion: Problems and Policies of a World Power," in *The Age of Expansion: Europe and the World, 1559–1660*, ed. Hugh Trevor-Roper (New York: McGraw-Hill, 1968), 44.
5. Ibid., 61.
6. Ibid., 44.
7. Michel Pastoureau, *Black: The History of a Color* (Princeton, NJ: Princeton University Press, 2008), 103.
8. Ibid.
9. Ibid., 63.
10. The oak gall, or oak apple, appeared on the leaves of certain oaks in the spring, when the trees' sap solidified around invasive insect larvae. Ibid., 91–92.
11. Ibid, 103.
12. Anderson, *Hispanic Costume*, 189.
13. Ibid., 187. In this ensemble the contrast is tonal, but a floor-length Eisa version of this model has bands of ruched aqua silk velvet on oyster-gray satin.
14. Ibid., 207.
15. François Lesage, interview with author, June 2010.
16. Mary Cable, *El Escorial* (New York: Newsweek, 1971), 27, 46.
17. Le Boulevardier, "Soirées parisiennes: En six robes et un travesti, Mme Alice Cocéa fait *Échec à Don Juan*," *Le Figaro*, January 16, 1942.
18. Hubert de Givenchy acquired two of the costumes from Cocéa in the 1960s and conspired with Balenciaga's butler to arrange them on mannequins in the salon of Balenciaga's Paris apartment. The designer wept with delight at this surprise gift. Givenchy, interview with author.
19. Jouve and Demornex, *Balenciaga*, 332.
20. The word *farthingale* derives from *verdugado*; the original hoops were made from willow

saplings, and *verdugo* is Spanish for green wood. Anderson, *Hispanic Costume*, 208–209.
21. Cable, *El Escorial*, 69.
22. Ibid., 69–71.
23. Lenaghan, *Hispanic Society*, 234.
24. The armor has been preserved in the Real Armería at the Royal Palace by edict of Charles IV. Antonio Domínguez Ortiz, Concha Herrero Carretero, and José A. Godoy, *Resplendence of the Spanish Monarchy: Renaissance Tapestries and Armor from the Patrimonio Nacional* (New York: Metropolitan Museum of Art, 1991), 97–98.
25. Lenaghan, *Hispanic Society*, 204.
26. Claude d'Anthenaise, *Janine Janet: Métamorphoses* (Paris: Éditions Norma, 2003).
27. Cable, *El Escorial*, 120–134.
28. Ribeiro, "Fashioning the Feminine," 71.
29. Ibid., 72.
30. The French client (based in Dallas) negated this subtlety somewhat with her introduction of rhinestone strips at the hip and bodice.

RELIGIOUS LIFE

1. Hugh Thomas, *Rivers of Gold: The Rise of the Spanish Empire, from Columbus to Magellan* (New York: Random House, 2005), 81–82.
2. Adrian Shubert, *A Social History of Modern Spain* (London: Unwin Hyman, 1990), 147.
3. Although Franco tried to establish a Concordat in 1941, it was not fully adopted until 1953. See George Hills, *Franco: The Man and His Nation* (New York: Macmillan, 1967), 382–384, 414.
4. For Balenciaga's uncle as parish priest, see Miren Arzalluz, *Cristóbal Balenciaga: La forge du maître, 1895–1936* (San Sebastián: Nerea, 2010), 218; for Balenciaga's interest in becoming a priest, see Walker, *Balenciaga and His Legacy*, 15.
5. Eve Auchincloss, "Balenciaga: Homage to the Greatest," *Connoisseur*, September 1989, 166.
6. Snow and Aswell, *World of Carmel Snow*, 164.
7. Walker, *Balenciaga and His Legacy*, 15.
8. McDowell, "Quiet Revolutionary," 135.
9. Areilza, "Image of Cristóbal Balenciaga," 24–25.
10. Miller, *Balenciaga*, 26.
11. Thurman, "Absolutist," 60.
12. Bergdorf Goodman sketched the designs it purchased from couture houses. These documents often note fabrication.
13. Jouve and Demornex, *Balenciaga*, 370.
14. Claudia Heard de Osborne, quoted in Walker, *Balenciaga and His Legacy*, 35.
15. Michael Walsh, ed., *Butler's Lives of the Saints* (New York: HarperCollins, 1991), 316.
16. Xavier Bray et al., *The Sacred Made Real: Spanish Painting and Sculpture, 1600–1700* (London: National Gallery, 2009), 178.
17. Ibid., 178.
18. Regarding the color violet, Vreeland stated, "Suddenly you were in a nunnery, you were in a monastery." Vreeland, *D.V.*, 106.
19. Rt. Rev. Monsignor John Walsh, *The Mass and Vestments of the Catholic Church: Liturgical, Doctrinal, Historical, and Archeological* (New York: Benziger Brothers, 1916), 247.
20. Ballard, *In My Fashion*, 107.
21. Ruth Matilda Anderson, *Costumes Painted by Sorolla in His Provinces of Spain* (New York:

Hispanic Society of America, 1957), 146.
22. Patrick Lenaghan, *Images in Procession: Testimonies to Spanish Faith* (New York: American Bible Society and Hispanic Society of America, 2000), 25. The example in the Metropolitan Museum of Art (25.228a–c) is split in the front and back and closes with ties in order to dress the sculpture easily.
23. Ibid., 26. Lenaghan used the term *madrina* in conversation with the author, 2010.
24. Miller, *Balenciaga*, 28.
25. Bray et al., *Sacred Made Real*, 196.
26. Jouve and Demornex, *Balenciaga*, 319–321.
27. For use of watered silk in clerical garments, see Rev. John Abel Nainfa, *Costume of Prelates of the Catholic Church According to Roman Etiquette* (Baltimore: John Murphy, 1909), 32–34.
28. Anderson, *Costumes Painted by Sorolla*, 46.

DANCE

1. Alfonso C. Saiz Valdivieso, quoted in Sonia Rueda Pardo, "José Arrúe y Valle," trans. Julia Arnhold, *Auñamendi Eusko Entziklopedia*, www.euskomedia.org/aunamendi, accessed November 28, 2010.
2. Pardo, "José Arrúe y Valle."
3. Matteo (Matteo Marcellus Vittucci), *The Language of Spanish Dance: A Dictionary and Reference Manual*, 2nd ed. (Hightstown, NJ: Princeton Book Company, 2003), 192, 194, 202.
4. Roger Salas, "Spanish Dance Dress, Its Origins and Development," in *Dressed to Dance*, brochure for an exhibition and performance at the Corcoran Gallery of Art, Washington, D.C., and the Guggenheim Museum, New York, 2010, 8.
5. Ibid.
6. Ibid.
7. Ibid., 8–9. The *ballet clásico español* flourished in mid-century Spain with troupes such as the one led by the distinguished Pilar López, whom Oscar de la Renta saw in Madrid in the 1950s. He was struck by "her cobalt blue *bata de cola* dress with an emerald-green stole." Oscar de la Renta, interview with author.
8. Salas, "Spanish Dance Dress," 9.
9. Ibid.
10. Ibid.
11. Matteo, *Language of Spanish Dance*, 109.
12. Barbara Thiel-Cramér, Flamenco, trans. Sheila Smith (Lidingö, Sweden: Remark, 1991), 41.
13. Ricardo Molina, quoted in ibid., 34.
14. Bernard Leblon, *Gypsies and Flamenco: The Emergence of the Art of Flamenco in Andalusia*, trans. Sinéad ní Shuinéar (Hertfordshire, UK: University of Hertfordshire Press, 2003), 19.
15. Ibid., 31.
16. Thiel-Cramér, *Flamenco*, 51.
17. Ibid., 51–52; Paco Sevilla, *Queen of the Gypsies: The Life and Legend of Carmen Amaya* (San Diego, CA: Sevilla Press, 1999), 40.
18. Thiel-Cramér, *Flamenco*, 105.
19. Ibid., 106; Salas, "Spanish Dance Dress," 9.
20. Thiel-Cramér, *Flamenco*, 106.
21. *Vogue* photographed one of these dresses from her winter 1937 collection, its multiple tiers of black velvet cascading over a red taffeta underskirt, flashes of which would be revealed in movement. By the 1950s De Pombo was

living in Madrid and married to Balenciaga's favorite antiques dealer in that city. Givenchy, interview with author. De Pombo also held fashionable cultural salons and gave flamenco dance performances of her own.

22. Sevilla, *Queen of the Gypsies*, 186.
23. Ibid.
24. Ibid., 186, 222, 230.
25. Ibid., 263; Leblon, *Gypsies and Flamenco*, 88.
26. Thiel-Cramér, *Flamenco*, 109.
27. William Washabaugh, "Flamenco Music and Documentary," in *Ethnomusicology* 41, no. 1 (Winter 1997): 53-57.
28. Leblon, *Gypsies and Flamenco*, 98-99.
29. Matteo, *Language of Spanish Dance*, 29.
30. Salas, "Spanish Dance Dress," 10.
31. Matteo, *Language of Spanish Dance*, 200.
32. Ibid., 103.
33. Salas, "Spanish Dance Dress," 11.
34. Anderson, *Costumes Painted by Sorolla*, 172-174.
35. Salas, "Spanish Dance Dress," 8. See discussion of *faralaes* (flounces).
36. Anderson, *Costumes Painted by Sorolla*, 167.
37. Ibid., 168.
38. Ibid., 167.
39. Ibid., 171.
40. Ibid.
41. Marciano R. de Borja, "Galleon Traders and Merchants," in *Basques in the Philippines* (Reno: University of Nevada Press, 2005), 58-74.
42. Salas, "Spanish Dance Dress," 11.
43. Ibid.
44. Thiel-Cramér, *Flamenco*, 98.

THE BULLFIGHT

1. Ballard, *In My Fashion*, 107.
2. Anderson, *Costumes Painted by Sorolla*, 159-160.
3. Abel Chapman and Walter John Buck, *Unexplored Spain* (New York: Longmans, Green, 1910), 196.
4. Anderson, *Costumes Painted by Sorolla*, 161.
5. Francisco Montes, *Tauromaquia completa* (1836; repr., Madrid: Egartorre, 1994), cover.
6. Anderson, *Costumes Painted by Sorolla*, 160-161.
7. Ibid., 160.
8. Ibid.
9. Miren Arzalluz, "Cristóbal Balenciaga: The Making of a Work of Art" (master's thesis, Courtauld Institute of Art, London, 2004), 9.
10. Ibid.
11. *Harper's Bazaar*, September 1, 1939, 49.
12. "Great Ladies of Madrid Society," *Harper's Bazaar*, September 1948, 178.
13. Igor Uria Zubizarreta, interview with author, March 2010. The suit is in the collection of the Fundación Cristóbal Balenciaga in Guetaria, Spain.
14. Salas, "Spanish Dance Dress," 10.
15. Ibid., 11.
16. Gregorio Corrochano, "What Bullfighting Means?" in *Los Toros*, 56.
17. Juan Belmonte, the most celebrated bullfighter of his day, appeared on the cover of *Time* magazine on January 5, 1925.
18. Detailed descriptions of the Andalusian *majo* and *maja* appear in Washington Irving's *Tales of the Alhambra* (Paris: Baudry, 1840), 21. Balenciaga's personal collection of historical costumes was

donated to the Galliera, Musée de la Mode de la Ville de Paris.
19. Ernest Hemingway, *Death in the Afternoon* (1932; repr., New York: Scribner, 2003), 329.
20. After the death of d'Attainville in 1948, Esparza took over the designing of hats. See Miller, *Balenciaga*, 21.
21. Dale Fuchs, "Illuminating the 'Suit of Lights,'" *New York Times*, March 5, 2005.
22. For a glossary of bullfighting terms, see *Los Toros*, 7-13. The portrait of matador Luis Miguel Dominguín on page 185 shows his *coleta*. Dominguín, who rose to prominence in the 1950s, was as famous outside the bullring as he was inside. Romances with the American actress (and Balenciaga client) Ava Gardner and the Balenciaga house model China Machado further propelled Dominguín's star status.

REGIONAL DRESS

1. Agustín Balenciaga Medina, interview with author, September 2010. For a photograph of Balenciaga in Seville, see Jouve and Demornex, *Balenciaga*, 20.
2. Ballard, *In My Fashion*, 105-106, 113.
3. See, for example, costume historian and photographer Ruth Matilda Anderson's *Costumes Painted by Sorolla*, *Hispanic Costume*, and *Spanish Costume: Extremadura* (New York: Hispanic Society of America, 1951); and photographer José Ortiz-Echagüe's *España*.
4. Julián Gállego, "The Spain of Zuloaga," in *Ignacio Zuloaga: 1870-1945* (Bilbao: Eusko Jaurlaritza, Kultura eta Turismo Saila; Dallas: Meadows Museum, 1991), 75.
5. For information about Zuloaga's collection and museum, see Matías Díaz Padrón, "Ignacio Zuloaga the Collector," in *Ignacio Zuloaga*, 95-128.
6. A painting of Lucía Zuloaga wearing a Balenciaga suit exists in the Zuloaga Museum in Zumaia. For Lucía Zuloaga as a Balenciaga client, see Miren Arzalluz, *Cristóbal Balenciaga*, 216.
7. See books by Anderson for detailed descriptions of Spanish regional dress.
8. "This bulky silhouette strikingly repeats one seen in the Mátra, a mountain district of Hungary. Mátra girls preparing for a festival must finish their toilet in the open air, because with all their fine-pleated skirts and petticoats in place they cannot pass through the home doorway." Anderson, *Costumes Painted by Sorolla*, 68.
9. Ibid.
10. See Ortiz-Echagüe, *España*.
11. Anderson, *Costumes Painted by Sorolla*, vi.
12. Ibid.
13. Patrick Lenaghan, *In the Lands of Extremadura: Ruth Matilda Anderson's Photographs of Western Spain for the Hispanic Society* (New York: Hispanic Society of America, 2004), 17; see 11-19 for further information about Anderson's career.
14. Ibid., 12.
15. Anderson, *Costumes Painted by Sorolla*, 18.
16. Anderson, *Spanish Costume*, 119.
17. Trowbridge Hall, *Spain in Silhouette* (New York: Macmillan, 1923), 16-17.

18. Author's correspondence with curators at the Museo del Traje, Madrid.
19. See comparative examples in Jouve and Demornex, *Balenciaga*, 162-167.
20. Ballard, *In My Fashion*, 110.
21. Miller, *Balenciaga*, 54.
22. A *liripipe* was a long streamer that hung down on the sides of a headdress. "Renaissance Spain had abundant intercourse with central Europe," with members of the Spanish royal family marrying into the princely families of Germany and Hungary, as noted by Anderson, *Costumes Painted by Sorolla*, 68.
23. See similar examples of the *majo* cloak in a painting attributed to Francisco de Goya, *Majas on a Balcony* (1808-1810), in the collection of the Metropolitan Museum of Art (29.100.10).
24. Anderson, *Costumes Painted by Sorolla*, 9.
25. Ibid., 48.
26. Ibid., 57.
27. Ibid., 8.
28. Miller, *Balenciaga*, 56.
29. Anderson, *Spanish Costume*, 121.
30. See Eugenio Lucas Velázquez's *Study for a Portrait of Isabella II* (ca. 1860) in the collection of the Museo Lázaro Galdiano, Madrid (11552). The elaborate lace mantillas and embroidered shawls that formed part of the Spanish presentation at the Great Exhibition of 1851 in London brought a flurry of fashionable attention to these elements of Spanish national dress.
31. *Le Figaro*, May 14, 1941, quoted in Golbin, *Balenciaga Paris*, 45.
32. For a photograph of this ensemble see Edmonde Charles-Roux, *Théâtre de la Mode*, ed. Susan Train with Eugène Clarence Braun-Munk (New York: Rizzoli/Metropolitan Museum of Art, 1991), 130.
33. Ballard, *In My Fashion*, 107.
34. See illustration in *Vogue*, November 15, 1945, 116.
35. For a description of Basque dress, see Anderson, *Costumes Painted by Sorolla*, 79-86.
36. James Snowden, *The Folk Dress of Europe* (London: Mills and Boon, 1979), 138.
37. Ibid.
38. "The most breathtaking moment of Balenciaga's collection—intense Seville yellow sculptured by gravity." *Vogue*, April 15, 1965, 85.

BIBLIOGRAPHY

Anderson, Ruth Matilda. *Costumes Painted by Sorolla in His Provinces of Spain.* New York: Hispanic Society of America, 1957.

———. *Hispanic Costume, 1480-1530.* New York: Hispanic Society of America, 1979.

———. *Spanish Costume: Extremadura.* New York: Hispanic Society of America, 1951.

D'Anthenaise, Claude. *Janine Janet: Métamorphoses.* Paris: Éditions Norma, 2003.

Areilza, José María de. "The Image of Cristóbal Balenciaga." In *El mundo de Balenciaga: Palacio de Bibliotecas y Museos, Salas de la Dirección General de Bellas Artes.* Barcelona: Productoras Nacionales de Fibras Artificiales y Sintéticas, 1974.

Arzalluz, Miren. *Cristóbal Balenciaga: La forge du maître, 1895-1936.* San Sebastián: Nerea, 2010.

———. "Cristóbal Balenciaga: The Making of a Work of Art." Master's thesis, Courtauld Institute of Art, London, 2004.

Auchincloss, Eve. "Balenciaga: Homage to the Greatest." *Connoisseur.* September 1989.

Baer, Ronni, and Sarah Schroth, eds. *El Greco to Velázquez.* Boston: MFA Publications, 2008.

"Balenciaga—and the Art of Making Elegant Clothes." *Women's Wear Daily.* July 9, 1958.

Balfour, Sebastian. "Spain from 1931 to the Present." In *Spain: A History.* Oxford: Oxford University Press, 2000.

Ballard, Bettina. *In My Fashion.* New York: David McKay, 1960.

Baticle, Jeannine, ed. *Zurbarán.* New York: Metropolitan Museum of Art, 1988.

Beaton, Cecil. *The Glass of Fashion.* London: Weidenfeld and Nicolson, 1954.

"Behind Him and within Him—Lies Spain." *Life.* December 27, 1968.

Belmonte, Juan. *Juan Belmonte: Killer of Bulls.* Translated by Leslie Charteris. Garden City, NY: Doubleday, Doran, 1937.

Biddle, Margaret Thompson. "The Art of Dressing Well." *Woman's Home Companion.* November 1953.

Billeter, Erica. "Cristóbal Balenciaga, Fashion King in a Museum." *Annabelle.* July 1, 1970.

Le Boulevardier. "Soirées parisiennes: En six robes et un travesti, Mme Alice Cocéa fait *Échec à Don Juan.*" *Le Figaro.* January 16, 1942.

Bowles, Hamish. "The Balenciaga Mystique." *Vogue.* March 2006.

Bray, Xavier, Alfonso Rodriguez G. de Ceballos, Daphne S. Barbour, and Judy Ozone. *The Sacred Made Real: Spanish Painting and Sculpture, 1600-1700.* London: National Gallery, 2009.

Brown, Jonathan. *Velázquez: Painter and Courtier.* New Haven, CT: Yale University Press, 1988.

Cable, Mary. *El Escorial.* New York: Newsweek, 1971.

Carr, Raymond. *Modern Spain, 1875-1980.* Oxford: Oxford University Press, 2001.

Carter, Ernestine. *Magic Names of Fashion.* Englewood Cliffs, NJ: Prentice-Hall, 1980.

Charles-Roux, Edmonde. *Théâtre de la Mode.* Edited by Susan Train with Eugène Clarence Braun-Munk. New York: Rizzoli/Metropolitan Museum of Art, 1991.

Les chefs-d'oeuvres du Musée du Prado. Geneva: Musée d'Art et d'Histoire, 1939.

Cole, Alan S. "The Art of Lace-Making." *Journal of the Society of Arts* 29 (September 9, 1881): 774.

Colección de Trajes de España de 1777. Madrid: Casa de M. Copin, 1777.

Crow, John A. *Spain: The Root and the Flower; An Interpretation of Spain and the Spanish People.* Berkeley: University of California Press, 2005.

De Borja, Marciano R. *Basques in the Philippines.* Reno: University of Nevada Press, 2005.

Delgado, Maria M. *Federico García Lorca.* New York: Routledge, 2008.

De Marly, Diana. *The History of Haute Couture, 1850-1950.* London: B. T. Batsford, 1980.

Díez, José Luis, and Javier Barón. *Joaquín Sorolla, 1863-1923.* Madrid: Museo Nacional del Prado, 2009.

Dior, Christian. *Dior by Dior.* Translated by Antonia Fraser. Middlesex, UK: Penguin Books, 1958.

———. *Je suis couturier.* Paris: Éditions du Conquistador, 1951.

Domínguez Ortiz, Antonio. *Velázquez.* New York: Harry N. Abrams, 1990.

Domínguez Ortiz, Antonio, Concha Herrero Carretero, and José A. Godoy. *Resplendence of the Spanish Monarchy: Renaissance Tapestries and Armor from the Patrimonio Nacional.* New York: Metropolitan Museum of Art, 1991.

Emerson, Gloria. "Balenciaga, the Couturier, Dead at 77." *New York Times.* March 23, 1972.

———. "Monarch of Haute Couture: Balenciaga the Unsurpassed." *New York Times.* August 5, 1967.

Eulalia, Infanta of Spain. *Memoirs of a Spanish Princess.* Translated by Phyllis Mégroz. New York: W. W. Norton, 1937.

Evangelisti, Silvia. *Nuns: A History of Convent Life, 1450-1700.* Oxford: Oxford University Press, 2007.

"Exhibit in Geneva Authorized by Franco Government." *New York Times.* April 21, 1939.

"Famous in Spain." *Vogue.* August 1, 1951.

Fraiser, Kennedy. "On and Off the Avenue: Feminine Fashions." *New Yorker.* June 16, 1973.

Fuchs, Dale. "Illuminating the 'Suit of Lights.'" *New York Times.* March 5, 2005.

Gállego, Julián, and José Gudiol. *Zurbarán*. New York: Rizzoli, 1977.

Garafola, Lynn. *Diaghilev's Ballets Russes*. Cambridge, MA: Da Capo Press, 1998.

García Lorca, Federico. *Three Plays: Blood Wedding, Yerma, The House of Bernarda Alba*. New York: Farrar, Straus, and Giroux, 1993.

Giménez, Carmen, and Francisco Calvo Serraller, eds. *Spanish Painting from El Greco to Picasso: Time, Truth, and History*. New York: Solomon R. Guggenheim Museum, 2006.

Glynn, Prudence. "Balenciaga and *la Vie d'un Chien*." *Times* (London). August 3, 1971.

Golbin, Pamela. *Balenciaga Paris*. London: Thames and Hudson, 2006.

Grumbach, Didier. *Histoires de la mode*. Paris: Éditions du Seuil, 1993.

Guerra de la Vega, Ramón. *El Madrid de Picasso: Historia de la fotografía (1900–1910)*. Madrid, 2009.

——. *Madrid historia de la fotografía: La época antigua (1839–1900)*. Madrid, 2003.

Guía Museo del Traje. Madrid: Ministerio de Cultura, 2004.

Guillaume, Valérie. *Courrèges*. Translated by Lorna Dale. New York: Assouline, 2004.

Gyenes, Juan. *Ballet Espagnol*. Paris: Société Française du Livre, 1956.

Hall, Trowbridge. *Spain in Silhouette*. New York: Macmillan, 1923.

Hartley, C. Gasquoine. *A Record of Spanish Painting*. London: Walter Scott, 1904.

Hemingway, Ernest. *Death in the Afternoon*. 1932. Reprint, New York: Scribner, 2003.

Hicks, Ashley. *David Hicks: A Life of Design*. New York: Rizzoli, 2008.

Hills, George. *Franco: The Man and His Nation*.

New York: Macmillan, 1967.

Hommage à Balenciaga. Lyon: Musée Historique des Tissus, 1985.

Hughes, Robert. *Goya*. New York: Knopf, 2006.

Hung, Mei-Hsueh. "The Master of Lace: A Survey of Cristóbal Balenciaga's Use of Lace from 1937 to 1968." Master's qualifying paper, Fashion Institute of Technology, 2006.

Ibañez, Vicente Blasco. *Blood and Sand*. Translated by Mrs. W. A. Gillespie. New York: E. P. Dutton, 1919.

Ignacio Zuloaga: 1870–1945. Bilbao: Eusko Jaurlaritza, Kultura eta Turismo Saila; Dallas: Meadows Museum, 1991.

Irving, Washington. *Tales of the Alhambra*. Paris: Baudry, 1840.

Jouve, Marie-Andrée, and Jacqueline Demornex. *Balenciaga*. New York: Rizzoli, 1989.

Kamen, Henry. *The Escorial: Art and Power in the Renaissance*. New Haven, CT: Yale University Press, 2010.

"The King Is Dead." *Women's Wear Daily*. March 27, 1972.

Klensch, Elsa. "Balenciaga: Fashion Changer." *Vogue*. May 1973.

Kuhns, Elizabeth. *The Habit: A History of the Clothing of Catholic Nuns*. New York: Doubleday, 2003.

Lanchner, Carolyn. *Joan Miró*. New York: Museum of Modern Art, 1993.

Latour, Anny. *Kings of Fashion*. Translated by Mervyn Savill. New York: Coward-McCann, 1958.

Leblon, Bernard. *Gypsies and Flamenco*. Translated by Sinéad ní Shuinéar. Hertfordshire, UK: University of Hertfordshire Press, 2003.

Lenaghan, Patrick. *Images in Procession: Testimonies to Spanish Faith*. New York: American Bible

Society and Hispanic Society of America, 2000.

——. *In the Lands of Extremadura: Ruth Matilda Anderson's Photographs of Western Spain for the Hispanic Society*. New York: Hispanic Society of America, 2004.

——, ed. *The Hispanic Society of America: Tesoros*. New York: Hispanic Society of America, 2000.

Martin, Richard. "Balenciaga." *American Fabrics and Fashions*. September–October 1986.

Martin, Richard, and Harold Koda. *Flair: Fashion Collected by Tina Chow*. New York: Rizzoli, 1992.

Matteo (Matteo Marcellus Vittucci). *The Language of Spanish Dance: A Dictionary and Reference Manual*. 2nd ed. Hightstown, NJ: Princeton Book Company, 2003.

McColl, Patricia. "We Are All His Family." *Women's Wear Daily*. March 27, 1972.

McDowell, Colin. "Balenciaga: The Quiet Revolutionary." British *Vogue*. July 1989.

——. "Hommage à Balenciaga." *Country Life*. October 17, 1985.

Miller, Lesley Ellis. *Balenciaga*. London: V&A Publications, 2007.

Montes, Francisco. *Tauromaquia completa*. 1836. Reprint, Madrid: Egartorre, 1994.

Morris, Bernadine. "Salute to the Art of Balenciaga." *New York Times*. October 1, 1985.

Mosley, Charlotte, ed. *The Letters of Nancy Mitford: Love from Nancy*. Boston: Houghton Mifflin, 1993.

Nainfa, Rev. John Abel. *Costume of Prelates of the Catholic Church According to Roman Etiquette*. Baltimore: John Murphy, 1909.

Noel, Gerard. *Ena: Spain's English Queen*. London: Constable, 1984.

O'Higgins, Patrick. *Madame: An Intimate Biography of Helena Rubinstein*. New York: Viking Press, 1971.

Ortiz-Echagüe, José. *España: Tipos y Trajes.* Bilbao: Décima Edición, 1957.

Pacheco, Francisco, and Antonio Palomino. *Lives of Velázquez.* London: Pallas Athene, 2007.

Palliser, Bury. *A History of Lace.* London: Sampson Low, Marston, 1865.

Pastoureau, Michel. *Black: The History of a Color.* Princeton, NJ: Princeton University Press, 2008.

Payne, Stanley G. *Spanish Catholicism: An Historical Overview.* Madison: University of Wisconsin Press, 1984.

Petrie, Charles. *King Alfonso XIII and His Age.* London: Chapman and Hall, 1963.

Pochna, Marie-France. *Christian Dior.* New York: Overlook Press, 2008.

Price, Clair. "Stirring Odyssey of Spanish Art." *New York Times.* May 28, 1939.

Pritchard, Jane, and Geoffrey Marsh, eds. *Diaghilev and the Golden Age of the Ballets Russes, 1909-1929.* London: V&A Publications, 2010.

Puzo, Dante A. *The Spanish Civil War.* New York: Van Nostrand Reinhold, 1969.

Ribeiro, Aileen. "Fashioning the Feminine: Dress in Goya's Portraits of Women." In *Goya: Images of Women.* Edited by Janis A. Tomlinson. Washington, D.C.: National Gallery of Art, 2002.

Richardson, John. *A Life of Picasso: The Prodigy, 1881-1906.* New York: Knopf, 2007.

Robertson, Cordelia Biddle. "Notes from Spain." *Vogue.* June 1950.

Salas, Roger. "Spanish Dance Dress, Its Origins and Development." In *Dressed to Dance,* brochure for an exhibition and performance at the Corcoran Gallery of Art, Washington, DC, and the Guggenheim Museum, New York, 2010.

Savage, Percy. "Balenciaga the Great." *Observer* (London). October 13, 1985.

Sevilla, Paco. *Queen of the Gypsies: The Life and Legend of Carmen Amaya.* San Diego, CA: Sevilla Press, 1999.

Shubert, Adrian. *A Social History of Modern Spain.* London: Unwin Hyman, 1990.

Snow, Carmel, with Mary Louise Aswell. *The World of Carmel Snow.* New York: McGraw-Hill, 1962.

Snowden, James. *The Folk Dress of Europe.* London: Mills and Boon, 1979.

Stals, José Lebrero. *No Singing Allowed: Flamenco and Photography.* Barcelona: RM Verlag, 2009.

"They Remember Balenciaga." *Women's Wear Daily.* March 27, 1972.

Thiel-Cramér, Barbara. *Flamenco.* Translated by Sheila Smith. Lidingö, Sweden: Remark, 1991.

Thomas, Hugh. *Rivers of Gold: The Rise of the Spanish Empire, from Columbus to Magellan.* New York: Random House, 2005.

Thurman, Judith. "The Absolutist: Cristóbal Balenciaga's Cult of Perfection." *New Yorker.* July 3, 2006.

Tomlinson, Janis A., ed. *Goya: Images of Women.* Washington, DC: National Gallery of Art, 2002.

Los Toros: Bullfighting. Madrid: Indice, 1964.

Trapier, Elizabeth du Gué. *Catalogue of Paintings (Fourteenth and Fifteenth Centuries).* New York: Hispanic Society of America, 1930.

Trevor-Roper, Hugh, ed. *The Age of Expansion: Europe and the World, 1559-1660.* New York: McGraw-Hill, 1968.

Veillon, Dominique. *Fashion under the Occupation.* Translated by Miriam Kochan. Oxford: Berg, 2002.

Vickers, Hugo. *Cecil Beaton.* New Haven, CT: Phoenix Press, 2002.

Vreeland, Diana. *D.V.* London: Weidenfeld and Nicolson, 1984.

Walker, Myra. *Balenciaga and His Legacy.* New Haven, CT: Yale University Press, 2006.

Walsh, Rt. Rev. Monsignor John. *The Mass and Vestments of the Catholic Church: Liturgical, Doctrinal, Historical, and Archeological.* New York: Benziger Brothers, 1916.

Walsh, Michael, ed. *Butler's Lives of the Saints.* New York: HarperCollins, 1991.

Washabaugh, William. "Flamenco Music and Documentary." *Ethnomusicology* 41, no. 1 (Winter 1997): 53-57.

White, Palmer. *Elsa Schiaparelli: Empress of Paris Fashion.* New York: Rizzoli, 1986.

——. *The Master Touch of Lesage: Fashion, Embroidery, Paris.* Paris: Éditions du Chêne, 1987.

Wilcox, Claire, ed. *The Golden Age of Couture: Paris and London, 1947-1957.* London: V&A Publications, 2007.

Wilson, Elizabeth. *Adorned in Dreams: Fashion and Modernity.* Piscataway, NJ: Rutgers University Press, 2003.

The World of Balenciaga. New York: Metropolitan Museum of Art, 1973.

Zapata, M. Paz Ocio. *Museo del Prado: Los Grandes Maestros.* Madrid: Edmiat Libros, 2005.

CATALOGUE OF THE EXHIBITION

The following catalogue is arranged chronologically and reflects the best available information at time of publication. Designs by Cristóbal Balenciaga (Spanish, 1895–1972) precede comparative works by other artists and designers. Plate references may refer to studio sketches or drawings, house photographs, illustrations or photographs from the fashion press, or contemporary photographs of the objects on view.

WORKS BY BALENCIAGA

Evening dress, summer 1938
(see pl. 34 for alternate colorway)
Black silk taffeta, guipure lace, velvet ribbon
Los Angeles County Museum of Art,
gift of Mrs. Francis D. Frost, Jr. (M.58.12)

"Infanta" evening dress, winter 1939
(pls. 5, 30)
Ivory silk satin, black silk velvet
Atelier: Suzanne
Archives Balenciaga, Paris

Afternoon ensemble with dress
and bolero jacket, ca. 1939
Black wool crepe, black silk satin
Collection of Didier Ludot

Coat, ca. 1939 (pls. 89–90)
Black silk ottoman
Collection of Hamish Bowles

Evening dress, 1940 (pl. 207)
Black crepe
Archives Balenciaga, Paris

Dress, summer 1940 (pl. 163)
Brown cotton sprigged with moss roses
Chicago History Museum, gift of
Mrs. Clive Runnells (1967.217)

Theater costume, 1941 (pl. 76)
Black silk velvet, sequin-and-bead
embroidery by Ginisty and Quenolle
Worn by Alice Cocéa in the play
Échec à Don Juan at the Théâtre des
Ambassadeurs in Paris
Archives Balenciaga, Paris, gift of Alice Cocéa

Evening ensemble, winter 1943 (pl. 144)
Brown velvet, black embroidery and ball fringe
Galliera, Musée de la Mode de la Ville de Paris,
gift of Miss Agassir (GAL 1977.33.4a–b)

Evening suit, winter 1945
Black silk faille, black silk velvet,
black sequin embroidery by Bataille
Atelier: Suzanne
Mannequin: Jannine
Phoenix Art Museum, gift of Elizabeth Arden
(1968.C.341.A–B)

Evening bolero jacket, ca. 1945 (pl. 164)
Black crepe, metallic thread, paillettes
Archives Balenciaga, Paris

Evening bolero jacket, winter 1946 (pls. 136–137)
Blood-red silk velvet, jet and
passementerie embroidery by Bataille
Atelier: Claude
Mannequin: Marièle
Collection of Hamish Bowles

Evening dress, ca. 1946 (pl. 113)
Beige taffeta, metallic embroidery
and pearls by Lesage
Collection of Hamish Bowles

Day dress, winter 1947 (pl. 178)
Black silk bengaline, black velvet
Atelier: Lucia
Mannequin: Yvonne
Fine Arts Museums of San Francisco,
gift of Mrs. Eloise Heidland (1982.18.1)

Evening bolero jacket, winter 1947 (see pl. 139
for alternate colorway)
Ruby-red cotton velvet, black beaded
embroidery by Rébé
Atelier: Claude
Mannequin: Jacqueline
The Metropolitan Museum of Art, gift of
Jean Sinclair Tailer, 1964 (C.I.64.13.3)

Evening dress, 1948
Gray silk taffeta
Museum of the City of New York, gift of Mr.
and Mrs. Alexander Slater (79.15.18a–b)

Day suit, summer 1948 (pl. 31)
White linen, black lace trim
Atelier: Denis
Mannequin: Frédérique
The Museum at the Fashion Institute of Technology,
New York, gift of Doris Duke (72.81.20A–B)

Afternoon dress, winter 1948 (pl. 182)
Black wool, pink silk taffeta
Phoenix Art Museum, gift of Peggy Eliasberg (2002.7)

Cocktail dress, winter 1948 (pl. 39)
Rose peau de soie, black lace
Fine Arts Museums of San Francisco, gift of
Mrs. C. H. Russell (1983.63.9a–b)

Evening cape, winter 1948
(see pl. 183 for a similar example)
Black silk faille
Atelier: Denis
Mannequin: Colette
Archives Balenciaga, Paris

Hat, ca. 1948 (pl. 141)
Black and white straw
The Museum at the Fashion Institute of Technology,
New York, gift of Doris Duke (72.81.60)

Headdress, winter 1949 (pl. 116)
Black tulle by Combier, gold embroidery by Lesage
Atelier: Suzanne
Mannequin: Paule
Museo de Bellas Artes de Bilbao

Day suit, summer 1950 (pls. 194–195)
Mustard-yellow linen by Besson
Atelier: Henri
Mannequin: Michèle
Collection of Hamish Bowles

Evening dress, summer 1950 (pl. 18)
Black wool, taupe silk shantung
Atelier: Claude
Mannequin: Jacqueline
Phoenix Art Museum, gift of Mrs. Donald D.
Harrington (1968.C.504.A–B)

Afternoon suit, winter 1950
(pls. 175–176)
Black silk satin matelassé by
Raymond Castelain
Atelier: Claude
Mannequin: Claude
Archives Balenciaga, Paris

Coat, winter 1950 (pl. 84)
Fawn wool duvetyn
Atelier: Lucia
Mannequin: Huguette
Chicago History Museum, gift of Kathleen Catlin
(1986.402.1)

Evening coat, winter 1950 (pls. 62–63)
Burgundy silk velvet
Atelier: Denis
Mannequin: Colette
The Metropolitan Museum of Art, gift of
Mrs. Byron C. Foy, 1955 (C.I.55.76.26)

Evening dress, winter 1950 (pl. 171)
Black silk taffeta by Staron
Atelier: Claude
Mannequin: Colette
Archives Balenciaga, Paris

Evening dress, winter 1950 (pl. 78)
Champagne silk satin, pink tulle,
embroidery by Ginisty and Quenolle
Atelier: Lucia
Mannequin: Sylvie
The Metropolitan Museum of Art, gift of
Mrs. Byron C. Foy, 1953 (C.I.53.40.11a–b)

Evening dress, winter 1950
Ivory silk satin, brown silk faille, embroidery of
metallic braid, beads, and rhinestones by Métral
Atelier: Suzanne
Mannequin: Sylvie
The Metropolitan Museum of Art, gift of
Mrs. Byron C. Foy, 1953 (C.I.53.40.10a–b)

Hat, winter 1950 (pl. 61)
Crimson velvet, black ostrich feathers
Mannequin: Colette
Archives Balenciaga, Paris

Evening coat, summer 1951 (pl. 173)
Black silk taffeta
Mannequin: Colette
Collection of Hamish Bowles

Evening dress, summer 1951 (pl. 24)
Ivory silk, white beaded embroidery by Bataille,
pink taffeta bow
Atelier: Suzanne
Mannequin: Claude
Archives Balenciaga, Paris

Evening dress, summer 1951
White silk, black beaded embellishment
Atelier: Lucia
Mannequin: Jacqueline
Collection of Sandy Schreier

Evening ensemble, summer 1951 (pls. 1, 7)
Black silk organza, white cotton piqué
Atelier: Claude
Mannequin: Jacqueline
Philadelphia Museum of Art, gift of John
Wanamaker, Philadelphia, 1951 (1951.73.1a–d)

Cocktail ensemble with dress and jacket,
winter 1951 (pl. 77)
Black silk moiré, ivory lace, black velvet
The Metropolitan Museum of Art, gift of
Bettina Ballard, 1958 (C.I.58.50.4a–d)

Evening dress, winter 1951 (pl. 161)
Black silk tulle, satin cuir, sequin embroidery
by Ginisty and Quenolle
Atelier: Claude
Mannequin: Colette
Archives Balenciaga, Paris

Evening dress, winter 1951 (pl. 51)
Black and white cloqué organza by Lamarre
Atelier: Lucia
Mannequin: Mary
Les Arts Décoratifs, Musée de la Mode
et du Textile, Paris (RI 2007.216.1–3)

Evening dress, winter 1951 (pl. 118)
Black silk taffeta, black lace
Atelier: Suzanne
Mannequin: Geneviève
The Metropolitan Museum of Art, gift of
Gina Gerardo 1993 (1993.393.2)

Evening dress, winter 1951 (pl. 130)
Black silk velvet by Jean Page, pink silk satin
Atelier: Lucia
Mannequin: Gisèle
The Metropolitan Museum of Art, gift of
Gina Gerardo, 1993 (1993.393.1)

Evening dress, winter 1951 (pl. 19)
Black wool, straw-yellow satin drape by Labbey
Atelier: Claude
Mannequin: Jacqueline
Galliera, Musée de la Mode de la Ville de Paris,
gift of Mr. Herbert-Georges Bigelow (GAL
1980.185.4a–b)

Day suit, ca. 1951
Black silk and wool worsted, black velvet
Collection of Hamish Bowles

Day suit, summer 1952 (pl. 192)
Red linen by Gerondeau
Atelier: Denis
Mannequin: Michèle
The Metropolitan Museum of Art, gift of
Bettina Ballard, 1958 (C.I.58.50.3a–c)

Evening dress, summer 1952 (pl. 167)
Oyster silk taffeta by Carlin,
black chantilly lace by Guibert
Atelier: Lucia
Mannequin: Michèle
Archives Balenciaga, Paris

Redingote, summer 1952 (pl. 92)
Black silk twill
Atelier: Denis
Mannequin: Héliette
Les Arts Décoratifs, Musée de la Mode et du
Textile, Paris, museum purchase (2005.137.1)

Evening dress, winter 1952 (pl. 16)
Black lace
Atelier: Claude
Mannequin: Michèle
Texas Fashion Collection, College of Visual Arts
and Design, University of North Texas, gift of
Claudia de Osborne (TFC 1981.022.001)

Eisa
Evening dress, winter 1952 (pl. 11)
Black wool jersey by H. Moreau et Cie, brown
tulle by Combier, ivory silk flower
Mannequin: Michèle
The Metropolitan Museum of Art, gift of
Mrs. T. Wynyard Pasley, 1978 (1978.71)

Cocktail hat, 1953 (see pl. 158
for a similar style)
Ivory silk satin
Collection of Sandy Schreier

Dinner dress, winter 1953 (pl. 179)
Black silk satin with chiné print of
white polka dots by Petillault

Atelier: Lucia
Mannequin: Missia
Collection of Sandy Schreier

Evening coat, winter 1953 (pl. 2)
Black lace, brown organza; worn with
white satin pants (ca. 1960)
Atelier: Suzanne
Mannequin: Solange
Victoria and Albert Museum, London, worn
and given by Baroness Philippe de Rothschild
(T.18A-1974)

Evening dress, winter 1953
Black wool
Atelier: Claude
Mannequin: Andrée
Collection of Hamish Bowles

Evening jacket, winter 1953
Ivory silk satin, embroidery by Métral
Atelier: Claude
Mannequin: Andrée
Collection of Marean Pompidou

Cocktail hat, ca. 1953
Black silk chiffon, pink silk rose,
black silk velvet flower
The Museum at the Fashion Institute of Technology,
New York, gift of Mary Connelly Graff and Jean
Connelly Mooney in memory of Eleanor Milburn
Connelly and Frances Milburn Lauck (98.146.24)

Cocktail hat, ca. 1953
Black silk velvet
Collection of Sandy Schreier

Evening dress, summer 1954
White cotton ottoman
Atelier: Claude
Mannequin: Yvonne
Worn by Hélène Lazareff
Les Arts Décoratifs, Collections de l'Union
Française des Arts du Costume, Musée
de la Mode et du Textile, Paris, gift of
Michèle Rosier in memory of her mother,
Hélène Lazareff (UF 74-33-4)

Cocktail hat, winter 1954
Black silk faille, yellow silk satin,
ostrich feathers, beads
The Metropolitan Museum of Art, gift of
Claudia de Osborne, 1977 (1977.407.9)

Evening coat, winter 1954 (pl. 95)
Black silk faille
Atelier: Denis
Mannequin: Yvonne
The Metropolitan Museum of Art, gift of
Countess Edward Bismarck, 1981 (1981.249.17)

Evening coat, winter 1954 (pl. 103)
Scarlet silk ottoman
Atelier: Denis
Mannequin: Nicole
The Metropolitan Museum of Art, gift of
Mrs. Byron C. Foy, 1957 (C.I.57.29.8)

Evening dress, winter 1954 (pl. 201)
Cerise silk faille
Atelier: Lucia

Mannequin: Maria
Les Arts Décoratifs, Collections de l'Union
Française des Arts du Costume, Musée de la Mode
et du Textile, Paris, gift of Madame Arturo Lopez-
Willshaw (UF 66-38-18 AB)

Eisa
Evening dress, winter 1954 (pl. 64)
Red velvet, faux-pearl embroidery by Lisbeth
Atelier: Claude
Mannequin: Mona
Texas Fashion Collection, College of Visual Arts
and Design, University of North Texas, gift
of Claudia de Osborne (TFC 1981.022.003)

Cocktail hat, ca. 1955 (pl. 134)
Black silk taffeta, crimson silk rose
Collection of Hamish Bowles

Evening dress, summer 1956 (pl. 35)
Ruched white tulle, black flowers
Atelier: Suzanne
Mannequin: Linda
Collection of Hamish Bowles

Evening dress, summer 1956 (pl. 157)
White taffeta with red chiné carnation
print by Abraham
Texas Fashion Collection, College of Visual Arts
and Design, University of North Texas, gift of
Claudia de Osborne (TFC 1982.028.001)

Eisa
Evening ensemble with dress and overskirt,
winter 1956 (pl. 168)
Black silk point d'esprit, gray silk faille
Atelier: Suzanne
Mannequin: Silvana
The Metropolitan Museum of Art, gift of
Inge Morath Miller, 1973 (1973.147.1a–b)

Evening dress, summer 1957 (pl. 198)
Red lace
Atelier: Claude
Mannequin: Tania
Archives Balenciaga, Paris

Evening dress, summer 1957 (pl. 200)
Red silk satin organza by Lajoinie
Atelier: Suzanne
Mannequin: Dany
Archives Balenciaga, Paris

Evening dress, summer 1957 (pl. 197)
Yellow lace by Marescot
Atelier: Lucia
Mannequin: Taïga
Archives Balenciaga, Paris

Evening dress, winter 1957 (pl. 132)
Black silk velvet, black silk faille
Atelier: Claude
Mannequin: Taïga
Collection of Hamish Bowles

Evening dress, winter 1957 (pl. 112)
Gold-embroidered brocade, pale-blue taffeta
Texas Fashion Collection, College of
Visual Arts and Design, University
of North Texas, gift of Bert de Winter
(TFC 1973.001.002)

Evening dress, winter 1957 (pl. 123)
Pink silk taffeta
Atelier: Lucia
Mannequin: Jenny
Museum of the City of New York, worn and
given by Mrs. Peter Baumberger (83.121.15)

Cocktail dress, summer 1958 (pl. 206)
Black silk shantung
Atelier: Lucia
Mannequin: Taïga
The Metropolitan Museum of Art, gift of
Mrs. Herbert Levine, 1973 (1973.196.1)

Day dress, summer 1958 (see pl. 99 for
alternate colorway)
Ivory linen by Staron
Atelier: Claude
Mannequin: Dany
Brooklyn Museum Costume Collection at
The Metropolitan Museum of Art, gift of
the Brooklyn Museum, 2009; gift of
Mrs. William Rand, 1971 (2009.300.31a–b)

Evening dress, summer 1958 (pl. 40)
Turquoise silk gauze by Lamarre
Atelier: Lucia
Mannequin: Arlette
Texas Fashion Collection, College of
Visual Arts and Design, University
of North Texas, gift of Bert de Winter
(TFC 1965.043.090)

Evening dress, summer 1958 (pl. 27)
White organza, embroidered and appliquéd
cotton roses by Lesage
Atelier: Lucia
Mannequin: Margareth
Archives Balenciaga, Paris

Cocktail ensemble with dress and bloomers,
summer 1959 (pl. 205)
Black silk dotted organdy
Archives Balenciaga, Paris

Evening dress, winter 1959 (see pl. 110
for fabric detail)
Ivory silk satin, "crown of thorns"
embroidery, rhinestones
Victoria and Albert Museum, London, worn and
given by Mrs. Charlton Henry (T.17-1974)

Cocktail dress, summer 1960 (pl. 120)
Ivory silk, polychrome silk floral
embroidery by Lesage
Mannequin: Margareth
Victoria and Albert Museum, London,
worn and given by Viscountess Lambton (T.27-1974)

Evening dress, 1960 (see pl. 79 for
a similar dress)
Gold silk satin, embroidery
Victoria and Albert Museum, London,
purchased and worn by Mrs. Fern Bedaux
(T.758-1972)

Evening dress, winter 1960
Yellow silk faille, polychrome embroidery
with thistle motif
Los Angeles County Museum of Art, gift of
Mr. James Pendleton (63.4a–b)

Evening ensemble with romper and
bolero jacket, winter 1960
Adapted from original design (see pl. 147)
Black silk charmeuse, pink silk faille,
pink silk *pampilles*, transparent beads
Mannequin: Dany
The Metropolitan Museum of Art,
gift of Baroness Philippe de Rothschild,
1973 (1973.21.6a–b)

Cocktail hat, ca. 1960
Black silk satin, black silk *pampilles*, black beads
Collection of Hamish Bowles

Hat, ca. 1960
Black silk scarf with pink dots by Sache
Texas Fashion Collection, College of Visual Arts
and Design, University of North Texas, gift of
Claudia de Osborne (TFC 1977.017.054)

Cocktail hat, 1961 (pl. 211)
Black silk organza
The Museum at the Fashion Institute of Technology,
New York, gift of Helen Gettler (94.67.1)

Cocktail hat, summer 1961
Black silk organza, black feathers
Mannequin: Marie-Hélène
Texas Fashion Collection, College of Visual Arts
and Design, University of North Texas, gift of
Claudia de Osborne (TFC 1980.014.031)

Evening dress, summer 1961 (pl. 122)
Black silk gazar by Abraham,
multicolored silk flowers
Mannequin: Marie-Hélène
Collection of Sandy Schreier

Evening dress, summer 1961
Fuchsia silk gazar by Abraham
Victoria and Albert Museum, London,
worn by Mrs. Stavros Niarchos and
given by Mr. Stavros Niarchos (T.26-1974)

Evening dress, winter 1961 (pl. 145)
Black silk cloqué, silk and jet-bead ball fringe
Atelier: Lucia
Mannequin: Ariane
Los Angeles County Museum of Art, gift of
Jane Gincig (AC1996.193.2.1–2)

Evening dress, winter 1961 (pl. 199)
Yellow silk linen by Abraham
Atelier: Claude
Mannequin: Taïga
Les Arts Décoratifs, Collections de l'Union
Française des Arts du Costume, Musée
de la Mode et du Textile, Paris, gift of
Maison Balenciaga (UF 69-10-13 AB)

Evening ensemble with dress and cape,
winter 1961 (pls. 54–55)
Lime-green silk gazar by Abraham
Atelier: Lucia
Mannequin: Godeline
Galliera, Musée de la Mode de la Ville de Paris,
gift of Paris-Musées (GAL 1992.89.Xa–b)

Cocktail ensemble with dress and cape,
summer 1962 (pl. 129)
Red silk taffeta with black dots by Ducharne

Atelier: Lucia
Mannequin: Dany
Galliera, Musée de la Mode de la Ville de Paris,
worn and given by Mrs. Antenor Patiño
(GAL 1979.14.1a–b)

Evening dress, summer 1962 (pl. 125)
Brown silk gauze by Sekers
Atelier: Lucia
Mannequin: Michèle
The Metropolitan Museum of Art, gift of
Florence Van Der Kemp, 1975 (1975.406.3a–b)

Evening dress, summer 1962 (pl. 73)
Gray cigaline by Bucol, bead embellishment,
gray bows
Atelier: Claude
Mannequin: Véronique
Les Arts Décoratifs, Collections de l'Union
Française des Arts du Costume, Musée de
la Mode et du Textile, Paris, gift of Maison
Balenciaga (UF 69-10-6)

Evening dress, summer 1962 (pl. 36)
Ivory silk gazar by Abraham, black lace
Atelier: Claude
Mannequin: Anna
Collection of Hamish Bowles

Evening ensemble with dress and jacket,
summer 1962 (pl. 209)
Black silk gazar by Abraham
Atelier: Suzanne
Mannequin: Taïga
Collection of Hamish Bowles

Day suit, winter 1962 (pl. 188)
Olive wool
Fine Arts Museums of San Francisco, the
Eleanor Christensen de Guigne Collection
(Mrs. Christian de Guigne III), gift of
Ronna and Eric Hoffman (1998.122.4a–b)

Evening cape, winter 1962 (pl. 150)
Black satin, pink silk *pampilles* by Lesage
Atelier: Lucia
Mannequin: Tamara
Archives Balenciaga, Paris

Evening dress, winter 1962 (pl. 196)
Yellow silk satin by Lajoinie
Atelier: Suzanne
Mannequin: Joséphine
Collection of Didier Ludot

Evening ensemble with dress and
bolero jacket, summer 1963 (pls. 107–108)
Oyster silk taffeta; polychrome embroidery
of silk, sequins, and beads; eyelet cutwork
Fine Arts Museums of San Francisco, bequest
of Jeanne Magnin (1987.25.5a–b)

Evening dress, winter 1963 (pl. 21)
Gray silk satin by Chatillon, Mouly, Roussel
Atelier: Suzanne
Mannequin: Anna
Archives Balenciaga, Paris

Evening dress, summer 1964 (pl. 127)
White silk satin organza with
black dots by Lesage

Atelier: Lucia
Mannequin: Margit
Archives Balenciaga, Paris

Evening ensemble with dress and cape,
summer 1964 (pl. 203)
Black silk gauze by Staron
Atelier: Suzanne
Mannequin: Dany
Los Angeles County Museum of Art, gift of
Mrs. Edward W. Carter (AC1996.183.5.1–4)

Evening ensemble with dress and jacket,
summer 1964 (pl. 96)
Black silk cloqué by Hurel
Atelier: Lucia
Mannequin: Annick
Archives Balenciaga, Paris

Tunic, summer 1964 (pl. 190)
Ivory linen
The Museum at the Fashion Institute of Technology,
New York, gift of Givenchy, Inc. (79.62.2)

Day ensemble, winter 1964
Black silk crepe by Staron
Atelier: Jacqueline
Mannequin: Emmanuelle
Archives Balenciaga, Paris

Evening dress, winter 1964 (pl. 68)
Silk tulle by Marescot, bronze and verdigris
bead-and-sequin embroidery by Lesage
Atelier: Ginette
Mannequin: Valérie
Worn by Mitza Bricard
Museo de Bellas Artes de Bilbao

Evening ensemble with dress and cape,
winter 1964 (pl. 210)
Black silk gazar by Abraham
Atelier: Lucia
Mannequin: Emmanuelle
Archives Balenciaga, Paris

Evening jacket, winter 1964 (pl. 148)
Black chenille by Rébé, aqua sequin
embroidery by Lesage
Atelier: Suzanne
Mannequin: Valérie
Archives Balenciaga, Paris

Evening dress, ca. 1964 (pl. 82), based on
a silhouette of 1954
Black silk velvet, ermine tails
Texas Fashion Collection, College of Visual Arts
and Design, University of North Texas, gift of
Claudia de Osborne (TFC 1978.013.015)

Evening jacket, summer 1965 (pl. 57)
Kelly-green silk faille
Atelier: Claude
Mannequin: Catherine
Archives Balenciaga, Paris

Evening wrap, summer 1965 (pl. 153)
Yellow silk, black silk satin bows
Atelier: Claude
Mannequin: Taïga
The Metropolitan Museum of Art, gift of
Countess Edward Bismarck, 1981 (1981.249.15)

Raincoat, summer 1965 (pls. 86–87)
Brown gabardine
The Metropolitan Museum of Art, gift of
Countess Edward Bismarck, 1981 (1981.249.1a–c)

Coat, winter 1965 (pl. 186)
Black Papacha mohair by Ascher
Atelier: Felisse, Lucia
Mannequin: Annick
The Metropolitan Museum of Art, gift of
Countess Edward Bismarck, 1981 (1981.249.4)

Dinner ensemble with dress and jacket, winter 1965
Black silk organza, cellophane, sequin embroidery
Worn by Countess Edward Bismarck
Museum of the City of New York, gift of the
Smithsonian Institution (86.25.4a–b)

Evening dress, winter 1965 (pls. 25–26)
Pink silk gazar by Abraham
Atelier: Lucia
Mannequin: Dany
Victoria and Albert Museum, London, given by
Miss Ava Gardner (T.435-1985)

Evening ensemble with dress and cape,
winter 1965 (pl. 105)
Fuchsia silk faille
Los Angeles County Museum of Art, gift
of the Estate of Mrs. John Jewett Garland
(M.71.19.5a–b)

Hat, ca. 1965
Blue silk
Worn by Princess Lilian of Belgium
Collection of Hamish Bowles

Beret, summer 1966
Red wool
Worn by Princess Lilian of Belgium
Collection of Hamish Bowles

Beret, summer 1966
White wool
Mannequin: Michèle
Worn by Princess Lilian of Belgium
Collection of Hamish Bowles

Cocktail dress, summer 1966 (pl. 154)
Fuchsia silk shantung, black lace, black
silk satin ribbons
Fine Arts Museums of San Francisco, the Eleanor
Christensen de Guigne Collection (Mrs. Christian
de Guigne III), gift of Ronna and Eric Hoffman
(1985.44.429a–b)

Cocktail hat, summer 1966 (pl. 74)
Pink silk organza, pink ostrich feathers,
rhinestone brooch
Mannequin: Liliane
Texas Fashion Collection, College of
Visual Arts and Design, University
of North Texas, gift of Claudia de Osborne
(TFC 1978.013.021)

Evening dress, summer 1966 (pl. 131)
Black silk gazar by Abraham, black silk
organza by Bianchini et Férier
Atelier: Lucia
Mannequin: Mike
Archives Balenciaga, Paris

Evening ensemble with dress and jacket,
summer 1966 (pl. 152)
Black Ziberline by Staron, pink silk
gazar by Abraham
Atelier: Suzanne
Mannequin: Mike
Fine Arts Museums of San Francisco,
the Eleanor Christensen de Guigne
Collection (Mrs. Christian de Guigne III),
gift of Ronna and Eric Hoffman,
1985.44.214a–b

Evening dress, summer 1967 (pls. 42–43)
White Ziberline by Staron, red silk taffeta,
red silk organza
Atelier: Lucia
Mannequin: Nina
Archives Balenciaga, Paris

Evening ensemble, summer 1967 (pl. 52)
Black silk gazar by Abraham
Atelier: Suzanne
Mannequin: Maria
Victoria and Albert Museum, London, given by
Mrs. Loel Guinness (T.39&A-1974)

Coat, winter 1967 (pl. 189)
Black wool by Prudhomme
Atelier: Suzanne
Mannequin: Taïga
Archives Balenciaga, Paris

Cocktail dress, winter 1967 (pl. 59)
Black silk gazar by Abraham, rhinestones,
faux pearls
Atelier: Lucia
Mannequin: Valéria
Archives Baleniciaga, Paris

Cocktail dress, winter 1967 (pl. 67)
Yellow silk cloqué lamé
Atelier: Felissa, Lucia
Mannequin: Taïga
Archives Balenciaga, Paris

Evening dress, winter 1967 (pl. 93)
Black silk velvet, rhinestone-and-
bead embroidery by Rébé
Atelier: Suzanne
Mannequin: Valérie
Worn by Kitty Carlisle Hart
Collection of Hamish Bowles

Evening dress, winter 1967 (pl. 208)
Black silk crepe
Collection of Hamish Bowles

Evening dress, winter 1967 (pl. 56)
Lime-green silk gazar by Abraham
Atelier: Lucia
Mannequin: Devi
The Metropolitan Museum of Art, gift of
M. Fairfax, 1995 (1995.446)

Evening ensemble with dress and
"chou" wrap, winter 1967 (pl. 47)
Black silk crepe, black silk gazar
by Abraham
Atelier: Lucia
Mannequin: Annick
Archives Balenciaga, Paris

Eisa
Cocktail hat, winter 1967
Black silk gazar by Abraham, rhinestones
Mannequin: Annick
Collection of Hamish Bowles

Evening dress, summer 1968 (pl. 48)
Navy blue silk gazar by Abraham, white organdy
Atelier: Suzanne
Mannequin: Danielle
Collection of Hamish Bowles

Evening ensemble with dress and capelet,
summer 1968 (pl. 101)
Deep-blue silk gazar by Abraham
Atelier: Lucia
Mannequin: Valérie
The Museum at the Fashion Institute of Technology,
New York, gift of Nancy Zeckendorf (86.66.4A–B)

Wedding dress and veil, summer 1968 (pl. 100)
White silk satin organza, silk gazar by Abraham
Private collection

Eisa
Hat, summer 1968 (pl. 102)
White linen by H. Moreau et Cie
Atelier: Ginette
Mannequin: Danielle
Collection of Hamish Bowles

ALSO ON VIEW

Processional banner
Spain, 17th century
Blue silk velvet, red silk embroidery,
silver-gilt braid
The Hispanic Society of America, New York (H7)

Chasuble (pl. 106)
Spain, 1725-1775
Linen, silk, metal thread
Fine Arts Museums of San Francisco, gift of
Archer M. Huntington (1934.3.241)

Processional banner
Spain, 18th century
Ruby silk velvet, gold embroidery
The Hispanic Society of America, New York (H1)

Goyesca maja costume (pl. 46)
Spain, ca. 1801
Light yellow silk bodice, yellow silk satin
skirt, black pom-pom net overskirt
Museo del Traje. CIPE (Costume
Museum, Centre for the Research of
the Ethnographical Heritage), Madrid
(CE009251, CE009305)

Virgin (Imagen de vestir) (pl. 115)
Spain, ca. 1825
Polychrome wood, costume and cape with
gadroon and gilt-foil thread embroidery and
sequins, gilt-metal nimbus, silver crown
The Hispanic Society of America, New York,
gift of Loretta H. Howard in memory of her
mother, Loretta Hines, 1982 (LD520)

Galician peasant costume from Lugo
Spain, second half of the 19th century

Red printed shawl, wool skirt, cotton shirt
and petticoat
Museo del Traje. CIPE (Costume Museum,
Centre for the Research of the Ethnographical
Heritage), Madrid (CE006183, CE006180,
CE009306, CE006179)

Mantón de Manila (shawl)
Spain, ca. 1922
Silk, polychrome silk floral embroidery
The Hispanic Society of America, New York,
gift of Mary Ellen Padin, 2002 (LH2078)

Traje de luces (bullfighter costume)
Spain, first quarter of the 20th century
Deep-red silk breeches and jacket with black trim
Museo del Traje. CIPE (Costume Museum,
Centre for the Research of the Ethnographical
Heritage), Madrid (CE000180, CE000181)

Tapada costume from Vejer de la Frontera,
Cádiz (see pl. 166 for a similar costume)
Spain, before 1936
White cotton petticoat, black wool skirt
and mantle
Museo del Traje. CIPE (Costume Museum,
Centre for the Research of the Ethnographical
Heritage), Madrid (CE005100-102)

Eric (Carl Erickson, 1891-1958)
"Infanta" evening dress by Balenciaga (pl. 5)
Watercolor and gouache
Published in Vogue, September 15, 1939
Condé Nast Archive
Handcrafted frame provided by Eli Wilner &
Company, Master Framers, New York

ACKNOWLEDGMENTS

Hamish Bowles

The exhibition *Balenciaga and Spain* and this associated publication have been immeasurably enriched by many people who have guided me at every turn with their profound enthusiasm for the subject and the project. For their generosity—in lending masterworks and sharing documentation, knowledge, and memories—I am immensely grateful.

It was Oscar de la Renta, chairman of the board of directors for the Queen Sofia Spanish Institute, New York, who first approached me with the idea of curating an exhibition on the subject of Balenciaga and the influence of his native Spain on his work. I am profoundly grateful to Oscar for this irresistible invitation, which resulted in *Balenciaga: Spanish Master*, shown at the institute from November 2010 through February 2011, and also for his evocative memories of working for Balenciaga in Madrid in the 1950s, and for his own stylish vision and ideas for that exhibition. At the institute, my thanks are also due to president and CEO Inmaculada Habsburgo.

From the first moment that I suggested expanding on this thesis for the Fine Arts Museums of San Francisco's de Young venue, director John E. Buchanan, Jr., has expressed boundless enthusiasm for the project. His support and passion have been extraordinary. I thank his wonderful team, in particular Krista Brugnara, director of exhibitions; Jill D'Alessandro, curator of costume and textiles; Karen Levine, director of publications; and Suzy Peterson, executive assistant, for all of their help and advice.

I am grateful to François Pinault, founder of PPR; François-Henri Pinault, CEO of PPR; and Nicolas Ghesquière, creative director of Balenciaga Paris, for their immense generosity in opening up Balenciaga's extraordinary archives to us, enabling research and providing a unique loan of historically significant clothing and accessories. My thanks also go to Balenciaga's Lionel Vermeil for his great support. Balenciaga's archivist Gaël Mamine has been tireless in his work on behalf of this exhibition, and to him I extend my deepest thanks and appreciation.

The early enthusiasm and extraordinary subsequent support of Harold Koda and Andrew Bolton at the Metropolitan Museum of Art, New York, have been tremendously motivational and substantive, and I thank them both. I am also grateful to Pamela Golbin at Les Arts Décoratifs, Musée de la Mode et du Textile; Dennita Sewell at the Phoenix Art Museum; and Myra Walker at the Texas Fashion Collection for sharing their research with me. Dilys Blum at the Philadelphia Museum of Art; Kristen Costa at the Newport Restoration Foundation; Laurent Cotta at the Galliera, Musée de la Mode de la Ville de Paris; Nancy Davis at the National Museum of American History, Smithsonian Institution; Phyllis Magidson at the Museum of the City of New York; Valerie Steele and Patricia Mears at the Museum at FIT; and Claire Wilcox at the Victoria and Albert Museum have all been exceptionally gracious in sharing their Balenciaga treasures and documentation with me. Miren Arzalluz pointed me to the photographs of José Ortiz-Echagüe, whose work has proved a touchstone. At the Fundación Cristóbal Balenciaga, Igor Uria Zubizarreta has been profoundly helpful. Sandy Schreier has generously shared her own research materials.

Any Balenciaga scholar owes a great debt to Marie-Andrée Jouve, for many years the tireless guardian of the Archives Balenciaga, and I join their number.

A particularly rewarding aspect of this project has been to share the invaluable memories of some of Balenciaga's clients, colleagues, and friends, who have all brought his world so vividly to life for me. I particularly wish to thank Rosamond Bernier, Deeda Blair, Régine d'Estribaud, Sonsoles Díez de Rivera, Federico Forquet, Giuseppe Gazzoni, Hubert de Givenchy, François Lesage, Rachel "Bunny" Mellon, Mrs. Derald H. Ruttenberg, Babs Simpson, Susan Train, and Emanuel Ungaro for their fascinating insights over the years. I also owe a debt to Agustín Medina Balenciaga for his own informed perspective.

I am grateful to Anna Wintour for her indulgence when this project has at times diverted my attentions from my *Vogue* life. At *Vogue* I am also indebted to my assistants Lindsay Talbot, Iann Roland-Bourgade, and Stephanie LaCava.

On behalf of the Fine Arts Museums, we extend our deep gratitude to the lenders, without whom this exhibition would not be possible: Archives Balenciaga, Paris (Charlotte Schmidt); Chicago History Museum (Tim Long); Galliera, Musée de la Mode de la Ville de Paris (Olivier Saillard, Sylvie Lecallier); the Hispanic Society of America (George Moore, Mitchell Codding, Marcus Burke, Constancio del Álamo, Patrick Lenaghan, Noemí Espinosa Fernández); Les Arts Décoratifs, Musée de la Mode et du Textile (Éric Pujalet-Plaa, Caroline Pinon); the Los Angeles County Museum of Art (Sharon Takeda, Clarissa Esguerra); the Metropolitan Museum of Art (Emily Rafferty, Thomas Campbell, Mark Joseph, Chris Paulocik, Elizabeth Bryan, Jessica Regan, Shannon Bell Price, Joyce Fung, Bethany Matia, Emily Foss); the Museo del Traje (Irene Seco, Helena López de Hiero d'Aubarède, Juan Gutiérrez); the Museo de Bellas Artes de Bilbao (Javier Viar Olloqui, Marta García Maruri, Mercedes Briones Pastor, Silvia García Lusa); the Museum at FIT (Ann Coppinger, Sonia Dingilian); the Museum of the City of New York (Susan Henshaw Jones); the National Gallery of Art, Washington (Mary Levkoff); the Philadelphia Museum of Art (Timothy Rub, Sara Reiter, Monica Brown); the Phoenix Art Museum; Sandy Schreier; the Texas Fashion Collection (Dawn Figueroa); and the Victoria and Albert Museum, London (Lesley Miller, Oriole Cullen, Eleri Lynn, Suzanne Smith).

I would also like to acknowledge the following institutions, scholars, and friends for their guidance and support: Lynn Ban; Claudia Bauer; Princess Minnie de Beauvau Craon; Nele Bernheim; the Biblioteca Nacional, Madrid (Sergio Martínez Iglesias, Miguel Castillo Montero); Beverley Birks; Christophe Bolloré; Eric Boman; Katell le Bourhis; Coco Brandolini; Sarah Brown; Christie's (Pat Frost); the Cincinnati Museum of Art (Cynthia Aménus); the Condé Nast Archive (Leigh Montville, Aaron Siegel); Madison Cox; Amalia Descalzo; Deutsche Kinemathek, Museum für Film und Fernsehen (Barbara

Schroeter); the Elizabeth Sage Historic Costume Collection, Indiana University, Bloomington (Kelly Gallett Richardson); the Fashion Museum, Bath (Rosemary Harden, Eleanor Summers); Liz Goldwyn; Stephanie Guarneri; Susan Gutfreund; Carolina Herrera; the Indianapolis Museum of Art (Niloo Paydar); Carolina Irving; the Irving Penn Foundation; Martin Kamer; the Kent State University Museum, Ohio (Sara Hume); Risteard Keating; the Kunstgewerbe Museum Berlin (Christine Waidenschlager); the Kyoto Costume Institute, Japan (Akiko Fukai, Tamami Suoh); Christian Lacroix; Armand Limnander; Gianluca Longo; the Louisiana State Museum, New Orleans (Wayne Phillips); Didier Ludot; the Manchester Art Gallery (Miles Lambert); Jane MacLennan; the Mark Shaw Archive (Juliet Cuming); the McCord Museum of Canadian History, Montreal (Cynthia Cooper); the Metropolitan Museum of Art (Mia Fineman); the Ministry of Culture, Spain (Daniela Bosé); Isabela Moro; Vilma Muñoz; the Museo de la Moda, Santiago (Nathalie Hatala, Jessica Meza); the Museum of Fine Arts, Boston (Lauren Whitley); Deborah Nevins; Lorry Newhouse; the Newport Restoration Foundation, Rhode Island (Bruce MacLeish); Lars Nilsson; Ken Nintzel; Lewis Orchard; Palacio Real: La Real Armeria (Hon. Yago Pico de Coaña); Glenn Petersen; Marean Pompidou; the Rhode Island School of Design, Providence (Joanne Ingersoll); the Richard Avedon Foundation (Michelle Franco); the Rijksmuseum, Amsterdam (Bianca du Mortier); the Royal Ontario Museum, Toronto (Alexandra Palmer, Anu Liivandi); Ralph Rucci; Dominique Sirop (Robert Knapp); Jane Stubbs; Kerry Taylor; Charles-Antoine Van Campenhout; Hugo Vickers; *Vogue* (Megan Salt, Ivan Shaw, and the invaluable Joyce Rubin); Mark Walsh; Clair Watson; Gordon Watson; Judith Watt; and the Western Reserve Historical Society, Cleveland (Dean Zimmerman, Danielle Peck).

AR New York's dynamic team (Alex González, Raúl Martinez, and Satian Pengsathapon with Julie Tudor and Jamie Freedman) conceived the exhibition catalogue's innovative art direction. The Fine Arts Museums' copublishing partners at Skira Rizzoli (Charles Miers, Margaret Rennolds Chace, Anthony Petrillose, Maria Pia Gramaglia, Allison Power, and Kayleigh Jankowski) have handled our exacting deadlines with supreme flexibility, and at times the required dose of humor, to help realize this exciting publication. We are all exceedingly grateful to Elisa Urbanelli for her swift and skillful editing and to Leslie Ann Dutcher for invaluable assistance with rights and reproductions.

I would like to thank Lourdes Font for her many insights and her meticulous translations of French texts referenced in this publication. I would like to express our gratitude to our extraordinary team of interns: Alexis Anselmi, Julia Arnhold, Nicole Bloomfield, Sarah Byrd, Emily Rudisill, Emma Kadar-Penner, Alexandra Owens, and Katherine Gregory.

The exhibition *Balenciaga and Spain* and this publication would not have been possible without the contributions of my indefatigable research associates, Jennifer Park and Molly Sorkin, who have brought their profound knowledge, enthusiasm, commitment, and refined research skills into play at every turn. I am truly indebted to them.

INDEX

Page numbers in *italics* refer to illustrations.

252

PHOTOGRAPHY CREDITS

Plates 1, 16, 31, 78, 176: Richard Avedon, © The Richard Avedon Foundation; 2: Horst / *Vogue* / Condé Nast Archive, © Condé Nast; 3, 151: Henri Cartier-Bresson / Magnum Photos; 4: Lipnitzki / Roger Viollet / Getty Images; 5, 19: Erickson / *Vogue* / Condé Nast Archive, © Condé Nast; 6, 17, 38, 44, 97, 104: Scala / Art Resource, NY; 7: Bill Brandt / Getty Images; 8, 18, 21, 24–26, 33, 35, 40, 42–43, 45, 51, 55–57, 64, 67–68, 73, 86–87, 91, 95–96, 99–100, 103, 112, 120, 122, 125, 129, 131–132, 139, 145, 147–148, 150, 153, 156, 161, 168, 171, 173, 175, 179, 186, 189, 196–201, 203–206, 208: courtesy of Archives Balenciaga, Paris; 9, 121, 126, 142, 160, 166, 170, 174, 177, 184, 187: José Ortiz-Echagüe, courtesy of Fondo Fotográfico Universidad de Navarra, © 2010 Artists Rights Society (ARS), New York / VEGAP, Madrid; 10, 210: Tom Kublin, image courtesy of *Harper's Bazaar*; 11: Richard Avedon, © The Richard Avedon Foundation, image courtesy of *Harper's Bazaar* and Paper Pursuits; 12: Beaton / *Vogue* / Condé Nast Archive, © Condé Nast; 13: © Estate of Graham Sutherland, courtesy of the Helena Rubinstein Foundation; 14: courtesy of the Irene Lewisohn Costume Reference Library, The Costume Institute, The Metropolitan Museum of Art, image copyright © The Metropolitan Museum of Art / Art Resource, NY; 15, 109: image copyright © The Metropolitan Museum of Art / Art Resource, NY; 20, 23, 60, 80, 94, 98, 202: Erich Lessing / Art Resource, NY; 22, 183: Coffin / *Vogue* / Condé Nast Archive, © Condé Nast; 27, 164, 207: Armelle Kergall, courtesy of Archives Balenciaga, Paris; 28, 124: The Bridgeman Art Library; 29: Gerard Blot, Réunion des Musées Nationaux / Art Resource, NY; 30: George Hoyningen-Heune, © R. J. Horst; 32, 65–66, 111, 114–115, 119, 135, 149, 162, 165, 172, 180: courtesy of The Hispanic Society of America, New York; 34: Eugène Rubin, image courtesy of the Fashion Institute of Technology I SUNY, FIT Library Dept. of Special Collections and FIT Archives; 36: courtesy of the Cecil Beaton Studio Archive at Sotheby's; 37: © National Gallery, London / Art Resource, NY; 39, 88, 106–108, 152, 154, 178, 188: Joseph McDonald, © Fine Arts Museums of San Francisco; 41: image courtesy of the Board of Trustees, National Gallery of Art, Washington; 46, 181, 185: courtesy of the Museo del Traje, Centro de Investigación del Patrimonio Etnológico, Madrid; 47: *Evening Dress with "chou" wrap (Sue Murray), Paris, 1967*, photograph by Irving Penn, copyright © 1967 Condé Nast Publications Inc.; 48: Newton / *Vogue* / Condé Nast Archive, © Condé Nast; 49: image copyright © The Metropolitan Museum of Art / Art Resource, NY, © 2010 Estate of Pablo Picasso / Artists Rights Society (ARS), NY; 50: Bridgeman-Giraudon / Art Resource, NY, © 2010 Estate of Pablo Picasso / Artists Rights Society (ARS), NY; 52: Bailey / *Vogue* / Condé Nast Archive, © Condé Nast, courtesy of David Bailey; 53: Kenny Komer, © 2010 Successió Miró / Artists Rights Society (ARS), New York / ADAGP, Paris; 54, 74, 102, 127: film by Tom Kublin, video courtesy of the Museum Bellerive, Zurich; 58: Philippe Migeat, CNAC / MNAM /Dist. Réunion des Musées Nationaux /

Art Resource, NY, © 2010 Successió Miró / Artists Rights Society (ARS), New York / ADAGP, Paris; 59: courtesy of HIRO; 61: *Winter Beret, Paris, 1950*, photograph by Irving Penn, copyright © 1950 Les Éditions Condé Nast S.A., courtesy of Régine d'Estribaud; 62: illustration Gruau © René Gruau SARL Paris (www.renegruau.com); 63: illustration Gruau © René Gruau SARL Paris (www.renegruau.com), courtesy of Les Éditions Jalou "L'Officiel"; 69, 116: photo Pottier, © Les Éditions Jalou "L'Officiel"; 70–71: photo Les Arts Décoratifs, Paris / Jean Tholance; 72: Giraudon / The Bridgeman Art Library; 75: Nimatallah / Art Resource, NY; 76: © International Center of Photography, David Seidner Archive; 77, 118: Clarke / *Vogue* / Condé Nast Archive, © Condé Nast; 79, 82, 157: Michael and Rosalyn Bodycomb, New York; 81: © Patrimonio Nacional, Spain; 83: Elke Estel / Hans-Peter Klut, Bildarchiv Preussischer Kulturbesitz / Art Resource, NY; 84: *Balenciaga Mantle Coat (Lisa Fonssagrives-Penn), Paris, 1950*, photograph by Irving Penn, copyright © 1950 (renewed 1978) Condé Nast Publications Inc.; 85, 113, 128, 134, 137, 146: Kenny Komer; 89–90, 195: Joseph McDonald, courtesy of the Fine Arts Museums of San Francisco; 91: Robert L. Bracklow, © Photo Collection Alexander Alland, Sr. / Corbis; 93: photo Guégan, © Les Éditions Jalou "L'Officiel"; 101: Neal Barr; 105: digital image © 2009 Museum Associates / LACMA / Art Resource, NY; 110: Hamish Bowles; 117: Roger Wood / Hulton Archive / Getty Images; 123: Bouché / *Vogue* / Condé Nast Archive, © Condé Nast; 130: Gjon Mili / Time & Life Pictures / Getty Images; 133, 169: The Bridgeman Art Library, © Artists Rights Society (ARS), New York / VEGAP, Madrid; 136: Bérard / *Vogue* / Condé Nast Archive, © Condé Nast; 138: James Burke / Time & Life Pictures / Getty Images; 140: Erich Lessing / Art Resource, NY, © Artists Rights Society (ARS), New York / VEGAP, Madrid; 141, 190, 211: © The Museum at FIT; 143–144: © Stéphane Piera / Galliera / Roger-Viollet; 155: © Marcelo Del Pozo / Reuters / Corbis; 158: Rawlings / *Vogue* / Condé Nast Archive, © Condé Nast; 159: Loomis Dean / Time Life Pictures / Getty Images; 163: Leonor Fini, © 2010 Artists Rights Society (ARS), New York / ADAGP, Paris, image courtesy of *Harper's Bazaar*; 167: © Karen Radkai / courtesy of Empire Editions; 182: courtesy of the Phoenix Art Museum; 191: Louise Dahl-Wolfe, Collection Center for Creative Photography, University of Arizona, © 1989 Arizona Board of Regents; 192: Horst P. Horst, © Condé Nast Archive / Corbis; 193: Tino Soriano / National Geographic / Getty Images; 194: © Norman Parkinson Ltd., courtesy of Norman Parkinson Archive and *Vogue* / The Condé Nast Publications Ltd.; 209: Draz / *Vogue* / Condé Nast Archive, © Condé Nast